Training in the Knowledge Economy

Professor Jim Stewart

Dr Carole Tansley

The Chartered Institute of Personnel and Development is the leading publisher of books and reports for personnel and training professionals, students, and all those concerned with the effective management and development of people at work. For full details of all our titles, please contact the Publishing Department:

Tel: 020 8263 3387
Fax: 020 8263 3850

E-mail: publish@cipd.co.uk

The catalogue of all CIPD titles can be viewed on the CIPD website:
www.cipd.co.uk/publications

Training in the Knowledge Economy

Professor Jim Stewart

Dr Carole Tansley

Nottingham Business School, Nottingham Trent University

© Chartered Institute of Personnel and Development 2002

First published 2002

Cover design by Curve
Designed and typeset by Beacon GDT
Printed in Great Britain by Short Run Press

British Library Cataloguing in Publication Data
A catalogue record for this book is available from the British Library

ISBN 0 85292 959 5

Chartered Institute of Personnel and Development,
CIPD House, Camp Road, London SW19 4UX

Tel: 020 8971 9000
Fax: 020 8263 3333
Website: www.cipd.co.uk

Incorporated by Royal Charter. Registered charity no. 1079797.

Contents

Foreword

Much has been written about the shift from a manufacturing to a knowledge economy. Technology alone has had a major impact on the way people work, and consequently how they are trained and developed. The need for the training profession to embrace these changes – particularly such technology-driven phenomena as e-learning – is heard again and again at conferences and in the media.

But what factors have the biggest impact on the training profession and how should training professionals, employers and government respond? To explore these issues, the CIPD decided to support a research project pulling together published evidence of changes to the training profession in response to the needs of the knowledge economy. The purpose of the research was to better understand how changes in the economy are influencing training and development practice in the UK, and how these changes might develop in the future.

It appears that we are in the early stages of a transition to a different kind of role for trainers. This can seem overwhelming to the profession, but it also holds great promise. The building of knowledge networks and the creation of learning opportunities are now central to organisational strategy. Training and development professionals are now in a position to fundamentally influence the way their organisations do business.

To do this, an understanding of the key issues affecting the profession is crucial. Specifically, what changes have there been in individual and organisational learning? What new training specialisms are being developed as a result? What are the major perspectives on the role of training in the knowledge economy, and where are the gaps and biases in current research?

An important concern is the problem of who takes responsibility for learning. Organisations are putting more responsibility for learning onto employees. But the research shows that employees exhibit low levels of motivation to manage their own learning. This problem is exacerbated by a lack of support from line managers. Low-skilled employees are particularly reliant on learning opportunities provided by their organisations – without support the result could be a learning gap that no one steps in to fill, with disturbing consequences for all.

Another major issue that emerges from the research is the importance of general managers in determining the climate for learning in organisations. The knowledge economy requires a much more strategic integration of learning into business processes, with much broader involvement from managers and others in the organisation. Training specialists will need to provide the expertise that makes this transition possible. Another key issue to emerge is the importance of social capital as a necessary element in promoting learning in organisations – necessary for building relationships where sharing knowledge is encouraged, and supporting alternative modes of learning in the workplace.

The research suggests that to succeed in the knowledge economy, training and development professionals will need to be able to do the following:

- encourage informal and social learning in the workplace

- build collaborative learning networks and social capital within organisations, but also with strategic partners

◼ address the issue of learner motivation

◼ engage senior and line managers in the learning process by disseminating the message of how people learn

◼ work together with employers and government to support new approaches to learning.

Continuous learning within the profession will be essential in meeting these challenges. This report lays the groundwork for further research into these and other areas, but many questions remain. The CIPD is looking to support future research that will explore how organisations are trying to address the new challenges identified here.

Jennifer Schramm

Adviser, Learning, Training and Development
Chartered Institute of Personnel and Development

Executive summary

This report explores the impact on the training function of the shift to a knowledge economy. It distinguishes the *knowledge economy* from the *new economy*. Specifically, the knowledge economy focuses on the importance of know-how, innovation, design and branding, and the social processes that create these, to the generation of a firm's competitive advantage, whereas the new economy refers to the transformation of economic activities as digital technologies make accessing, processing and storing information increasingly more efficient. The report identifies a range of issues that will have significant impact on the role of training in the knowledge economy:

◘ Responsibility for learning and development is increasingly being placed on managers and employees rather than training professionals. This has implications for the role of the training contribution, with more importance attached to acting as learning *facilitator* and strategic partner rather than training *provider*.

◘ It is unsafe to assume that managers and other employees possess either the necessary competence or that they will adopt positive attitudes towards their new responsibilities.

◘ The immediate and medium-term contribution of training and training professionals therefore needs to focus on developing the competence and motivation of managers and other employees in relation to managing learning and development. Training professionals must play a crucial role in changing the organisational culture to one where line managers understand and act on their responsibility to support the learning and development of the employees whom they manage.

◘ Informal and work-based learning is of increasing importance in the knowledge economy. Highly developed learning skills are necessary to maximise the potential offered by conscious and deliberate learning through work.

◘ Developing these skills in the workforce requires training practitioners to concentrate their attention on learning *processes* rather than the *content* of learning much more than in the past. Effective learning process design will make a significant contribution to developing the skills of learning.

◘ This supports an idea that many training professionals have been advocating, that is of the trainer as facilitator rather than instructor. This may be particularly true when dealing with knowledge workers who are themselves subject specialists and who are highly demanding of training.

◘ Learning processes that utilise approaches made possible by developments in information and communication technologies (ICT), referred to as 'e-learning', require particular attention.

◘ 'Blended' solutions, which combine the best practices in e-learning and non-ICT approaches, may be more effective than solutions based exclusively on e-learning.

◘ Significant structural and cultural barriers to both formal and informal learning exist in work organisations. These barriers contribute to low levels of self-motivation among employees to manage their own learning. Aligning employee and organisational goals and the removal of these barriers to learning are crucial for motivation to learn and equality of opportunity in learning to be achieved.

◻ The training profession cannot achieve the necessary adjustments to the knowledge economy in isolation. Changes in national vocational and educational training (VET) institutions and policies are also required. An over-emphasis on the supply side of the learning market, and the application of human capital theory, are leading to skills polarisation and associated problems with social cohesion. Organisational policy and practice reinforce these effects: for example, employers engaging in unequal distribution of training resources.

◻ Government and employers need to address barriers to learning in their policy interventions. In this, small and medium-sized enterprises (SMEs) should not be forgotten, so their context will demand particular rather than general responses.

◻ The concept of *social capital*, defined as the resources derived from networks of relationships, has potential value in dealing with the changing role of training in the knowledge economy. The concept is relevant to understanding the dynamic of that economy and offers a way of analysing the contribution of training. The resulting analyses will be important in the continual development of training practitioners themselves to equip them to meet the challenge of their new roles. Related to this, greater understanding of group, organisational and individual learning as well as knowledge management is required. This improved understanding will also be a critical component in the development of training practitioners.

Much, though, remains to be studied and learned. This report provides a limited, though focused, snapshot of current knowledge on this topic. It identifies a focus for future research. The resulting research agenda should include studies dealing with human resource development (HRD) in the business environment, learning processes, the purpose and accountability of HRD, work organisation and design, and learning and individual identity.

1 | Changes in the business environment

◩ **Knowledge has become the most significant asset in achieving competitive advantage.**

◩ **With the importance of knowledge as its defining characteristic, the knowledge economy is a more accurate term than the 'new economy' to describe today's dominant economic environment.**

◩ **Globalisation and developments in ICT are the two most significant factors in the emergence of the knowledge economy.**

◩ **The knowledge economy is not defined by the emergence of 'dot.coms'.**

◩ **The emergence of the knowledge economy goes further than the changes in the proportional and relative values of manufacturing versus service industries in the economy. It has transformed the content and nature of production and consumption.**

◩ **The rise of the knowledge economy has significant implications for learning and training for and at work.**

The primary aim of this report is to establish, review and evaluate current knowledge and understanding of the impact of 'the knowledge economy' on the professional practice of training and development in the UK. The purpose of this chapter is to highlight the changes that have occurred in the recent past to the business environment.

In doing this, the meaning and nature of terms that have come into general use by managers, such as 'the new economy' and 'the knowledge economy' will be reviewed. It is suggested here that the term 'knowledge economy' is the more useful of the two, mainly because it is indicative of how the notion of knowledge is increasingly becoming a defining characteristic in seeking to describe and understand the changes occurring in the business environment and the organisation of work (a full glossary of terms appears as Appendix 2 to this report).

This discussion provides the context for the subsequent analysis of related changes in the organisation of work, individual and organisational learning, and the role of training and development. Some terms specific to the area that are emerging as worthy of consideration include: the notion of a learning society, lifelong learning, and social capital. The first two have obvious connections with the concept of the knowledge economy. The third is a concept that is gaining currency in both macro- and microanalyses of the economy because of its utility in understanding the connections between social relationships and economic outcomes. Each of these terms will be developed in later chapters of the report, so it will be useful to introduce them here in the context of our examination of the knowledge economy.

'One commonly held misunderstanding of the term "new economy" is the view that it describes the emergence of the "dot.com" companies...'

The new economy

The effects and consequences of globalisation (economic, social and cultural) and the rise in the use of information and communication technologies (ICT) are the two main components recognised as necessary in the creation of the new conditions that are referred to as 'the new economy'. One commonly held misunderstanding of the term 'new economy' is the view that it describes the emergence of the 'dot.com' companies and their impact in and on the economies of the developed world. In the World Employment Report (WER, 2001) it is argued that attention to what it describes as the 'volatile new world of the 'dot.coms' is a distraction, and evidence is provided to show that Internet companies cannot be justified as the defining characteristic of the new economy, especially given the posited reduction in this area. As demonstrated in a recent Oftel report (Cope, 2001, p17), Internet penetration in the UK has experienced a fall for the first time, from 40 per cent to 39 per cent. Given these issues, in this report attention will not be restricted to that sector of the economy.

A number of websites exist to enable thinking and debate about the new economy. One such site is to be found at http://hotwired.lycos.com/special/ene/ called the *Encyclopaedia of the New Economy*. Box 1 opposite contains an example of the sort of commentary it carries.

> **BOX 1**
>
> **An Internet 'Encyclopedia of the New Economy'**
>
> 'So what is the new economy?
>
> - communications technology creates global competition
> - innovation is more important than mass production
> - investment buys new concepts or the means to create them, rather than new machines
> - rapid change is a constant
> - at least as different from what came before it as the industrial age was from its agricultural predecessor
> - it is a world so different its emergence can only be described as a revolution
> - free markets are central to it. The Soviet Union's collapse settled the debate between market economies and planned ones.
> - the unprecedented power of global markets to innovate, to create new wealth, and to distribute it more fairly is to miss the most interesting part of the story. Markets themselves are changing profoundly....
>
> A final thing we don't know is where – or how – the revolution will end. We are building it together, all of us, by the sum of our collective choices. To help inform the architects of this new world, we've assembled an *Encyclopaedia of the New Economy*. Read on, pioneer.'

Two factors that appear to have an inordinate influence on the changing business environment are globalisation and developments in ICT, which in turn justify the notion of a new economy and which support the focus on knowledge. There are links and connections between them and there may be a synergistic relationship. However, the phenomenon of globalisation is much wider than that allowed by ICT. As Anthony Giddens amongst others argues, the compression of physical space through faster and cheaper travel is a key component of globalisation, as is the related global diaspora of various races and nationalities (see Field, 2000). So, while ICT enables the compression of time and space in relation to information and knowledge, other factors are also important in understanding globalisation. It is necessary, therefore, to examine each of the factors independently.

Globalisation

Globalisation is the term used to denote a growing interdependence of world society (Giddens, 1989). This growing interdependence arises, in part, from the compression of time and space in the everyday and lived experience of individuals across the world. The awareness of this compression, and the influence and impact of that awareness, is a further defining characteristic of globalisation (see Robertson, 1992). In economic terms, the breakdown of the Bretton Woods agreements – established after World War II as an attempt to manage the international financial system – in the early 1970s, and the subsequent and consequent liberalisation of the world's financial markets, is generally agreed to be a significant point in the growth and development of what we refer to now as globalisation. It is important to make this point because the phenomenon is in fact a continuation, though in intensified form, of a well-established historical trend of internationalisation (see Green, 2000).

As well as liberalisation of financial markets, a similar process of liberalisation of trade over the past 20 to 30 years has also fuelled the process. One result of this economic globalisation has been the rise to prominence and influence of multi-national corporations (MNCs). Those corporations illustrate that for economic actors – whether nation states, companies or individuals – globalisation is both an input and an output. The compression of time and space enables states, companies and individuals to operate in global markets, and therefore globalisation is an input into their decision-making. However, that compression is also the result of decisions made by those same actors: individuals working in companies lobbying for the liberalisation of world trade in goods and services and governments deciding to respond, for example. Therefore, globalisation is also an output of the decisions of economic actors.

While the economic causes and effects of globalisation receive most attention, it is important to recognise that the process has social and cultural dimensions (see Ritzer, 2000). The latter manifests itself most clearly in terms of food, films, television, etc and the argued American (or Western at least) hegemony in cultural tastes and practices across the world. However, these dimensions are more useful as analytical frameworks than as accurate reflections of lived experience. Naomi Klein's book *No Logo* (2000) on the impact of brands and branding demonstrates the close relationship between cultural and economic globalisation, as does the recent EC report on employment in cultural industries (European Commission, 2001).

The impact of ICT

Developments in ICT, and the close association with the development and management of knowledge, are highly significant in relation to those new conditions that are deemed important for the development of the new economy. As Leadbeater (2000) argues, the generation, application and exploitation of knowledge are driving modern economic growth, and if we

> **'As a vehicle for creating and sustaining human capital, self-directed learning is clearly very important.'**

ignore or seek to resist the globalisation of the economy, then we also ignore what he calls the 'most vital force in modern societies', and that is the 'accelerating speed of the spread of knowledge and ideas' (ibid). He cites Adams and Freeman (2000) as arguing that it is the emerging and developing capabilities of ICT that enable and facilitate the 'spreading' of knowledge. The World Employment Report (WER, 2001) also highlights the importance of ICTs, arguing that they will transform the 'old economy'.

The transformation of information dissemination

It is the ability to share, disseminate and exploit information and knowledge that will truly bring about the transformation; ICT is simply the enabler and facilitator. Two significant components of the transformation are identified in the WER (2001). The first follows from what the authors refer to as 'digital globalisation'. This term is useful in highlighting the connections between the two key factors identified in this chapter as driving the new economy. For the authors of the WER (2001), digital globalisation creates the condition that 'time to market' is now the critical competitive asset. The second component of the transformation is that work becomes independent of location. This component reflects the compression of time and space, which is a feature of globalisation. According to the report, it is also a practical outcome of the increasing capabilities of ICT – and the most significant of these is the Internet.

It is the Internet that allows work, of some types at least, to be independent of location. As the report notes, over one-quarter of all employees in the UK now carry out some of their work at home. More specific examples, including for instance music

production and distribution, are provided in a recent EU report (European Commission, 2001). Call centres are another example where work can be independent of location. The report estimates that 1.5 million people in the European Union (EU) are currently employed in call centres, with expectations of accelerating growth in the future.

Skills polarisation and quantity of work

The authors of the WER (2001) add some words of caution. They note for example that only 6 per cent of the world's population have ever logged on to the Internet. The work of Castells on the rise of the 'network society' stresses the role that technology plays in the creation of networks that can marginalise or exclude social groups or even entire nations. These networks reflect and create distinctive cultures, and because they exist outside national regulation and are hence politically unanswerable, enormous power lies in the hands of those who control them (Castells, 1996).

The WER also expresses concern about the number of jobs available in the future, especially for young people and new entrants to the labour market. Many authors, most notably Rifkin (1995), put forward the idea that there will no longer be enough work for everyone. Others stress the relocation of some kinds of work, mainly manufacturing, from one part of the world to another (Beaujolin, 1997). There may be disagreement about an end to work in its entirety, but there seems to be general agreement about the problem of under-skilled workers. They are most threatened by a knowledge economy where the only jobs created are in high-skilled, knowledge-based work. If there is to be an 'end of work', as Rifkin believes, it will start with low-skilled workers. Perhaps for this reason, recent CIPD research shows that lower-skilled employees

> 'Employees generally continue to work long hours, with schedules determined by their employers, in offices rather than at home, and the old barriers to success remain.'

are less likely to turn down opportunities to train than higher-skilled workers, who presumably feel more secure about their skills levels (CIPD, 2002).

Two other issues are also of concern. The first is growth in job and income insecurity associated with the changing nature of work. The second is gender inequalities in the distribution of work and jobs. The WER notes that two-thirds of the illiterate people in the world are women. Both of these issues are encapsulated in concerns about skill polarisation arising from the growth of the role of ICT in both product and labour markets (see Green, 2000). The European Commission (EC) shares these concerns about the availability and distribution of work and jobs (IPTS, 2000), and both the International Labour Organisation (ILO) and the EC have commissioned and are commissioning research into transitions into work and overcoming gender inequalities. On balance, though, the WER (2001) is optimistic on future employment opportunities and concludes that ICT does and will have more positive than negative effects in terms of job creation. However, ICT also has a major impact on the nature of jobs and how they are organised. The nature of that impact is signalled in part by the report's sub-title: 'Life at work in the information economy', an analysis which, according to the EC, is also true of Europe (European Commission, 2000).

Working life

While it is argued here that the new economy does not consist solely of the 'dot.com' sector, nevertheless, as a notable recent business feature, they do merit mention. The rise of 'dot.coms' seemed to signal not only a new way of doing business but also a new way of approaching work – one where the established notions of hierarchy, formality and bureaucracy were thrown away in favour of a networked, flexible and energetic

working environment where anyone with ability and ideas could succeed. But was this ever really the reality? When examined more closely, the 'dot.com' phenomenon has had little impact on working life. Employees generally continue to work long hours, with schedules determined by their employers, in offices rather than at home, and the old barriers to success remain. The next exhibit is an extract from *Dot Bombshell: Women, e-quality and the new economy*, published by The Industrial Society Futures Division (see www.indsoc.co.uk/futures). The implication in the article is that, in spite of claims to the contrary, the new economy is reproducing a similar élite profile to the old – a male-oriented one. (See Box 2, page 6.)

A similar situation is apparent in the wider 'new economy'. EC-sponsored research examined employment in the TIMES (telecommunications, Internet, multi-media, e-commerce, software and security) sector of the economy and found women to be under-represented. That this sector is significant for current and future employment growth is evident from Figures 1 and 2 (see page 7), which are taken from *Employment in Europe 2001* (EC, 2001).

Let us now turn our attention to a more detailed examination of work, organisations and employment characteristics of the knowledge economy.

The knowledge economy

One critical feature of the knowledge economy is the focused recognition on networks, both human and technological, and the necessity for and further development of innovative management techniques that help to deal with the challenges of what have become known as intangible

(cont. page 8)

BOX 2
No gender improvement situation in the dot.coms?

Has the exciting new world of the e-economy opened up vast new opportunities for women? Not really, says Helen Wilkinson. Despite the impression created in our national newspapers, the perception of many women in the [new media] industry and the success of a few highly talented women in e-commerce, the hard facts suggest there is no discernible difference between the working patterns of the old and the new economy.

Indeed, the early evidence suggests that women remain almost as under-represented in the new economy as in the old. The trends in the traditional economy are well known but worth restating. Women make up just 8 per cent of executive directors. An analysis of 1,178 directorships in the top 100 companies in the summer of 1999 showed that only 69 posts were held by just 61 women; and only eight were executive positions.

New economy trends are not radically different. And despite the high profile and attention given to the few dot bombshells that are scaling the heights of the new economy, there is no firm evidence to suggest that women as a group are more likely to set up an Internet business than any other. Of the hundreds of Internet firms founded across Britain each month, one in three has a woman behind it – directly paralleling the national statistics about female entrepreneurship in the economy as a whole.

Women involved in business start-ups suffer financing and resource issues and there is no reason to believe that the Internet industry is any different. Under-resourcing and difficulties in raising venture capital finance are common sources of complaint at many of the network meetings for women in the new economy. Female-owned businesses that clear the financing

hurdles and achieve rapid growth are few and far between.

There may be push-and-pull factors at work. Women may be less likely to seek venture capital finance, and in turn venture capitalists may judge the few women who do with suspicion. As one venture capitalist puts it, 'The truth is the vast majority of businesses we see are still founded by young, white, middle-class men. In terms of running projects or pitching for funding, I would say the split could be as high as 80/20 in favour of men.'

The figures certainly suggest there is some kind of drop-off as women scale the heights of the new economy. According to the regular surveys of the e25 published by *Management Today* in association with Bain and Co, only three women have been listed as founders, although those three have been placed high up the league. These are Sherry Coutu, who founded iii, Martha Lane Fox of lastminute.com and Caroline Williams of Freecom.net.

Other leagues produce similar findings. The *Guardian*'s statistics for the e50 showed that the average age was 34, and only 10 per cent were female, the average company age being 27 months. Those who are involved in the top echelons of the new economy tend to come from the dominant socio-economic group – white, male, Oxbridge-educated with contacts and confidence – thus challenging the anarchic outsider theory promulgated by writers such as Sadie Plant. And of the increasing number of Internet start-up billionaires, there is not one woman. The implication? The new economy is reproducing a similar élite profile to that of the old.

How do new economy businesses fare when it comes to female representation on company boards? Here again, under-representation is an issue. Among the three largest Internet companies – Freeserve, QXL and

Autonomy – there is only one woman director, and that is in a non-executive role.

Even in the USA, where the e-commerce industry is more mature, there are few Internet heroines. As in Britain, a few high-profile women grab the headlines.

Kim Polese, who invented the Java programming language before setting up her company, Marimba, is one example, but high-profile role models are not yet translating into critical mass. In the USA, less than 10 per cent of the business plans that venture capitalists receive are from companies with a woman at the helm.

Figure 1 | Employment in knowledge-intensive sectors in European countries, 2000 (share of total employment)

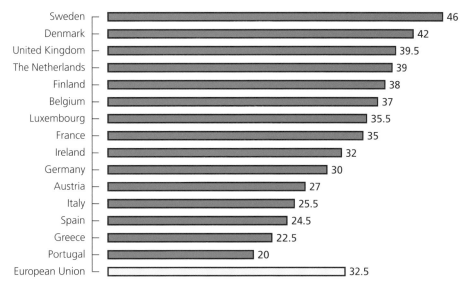

(*Source*: European Commission, 2001)

Figure 2 | Employment growth in high technology and other sectors, 1996–2000 (annual per cent change)

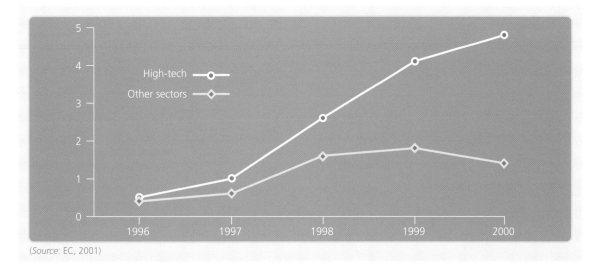

(*Source*: EC, 2001)

organisational assets. The knowledge economy has been described as the 'new' new economy by writers such as Juergen H. Daum, a specialist and consultant in enterprise management concepts and systems, with the actual focus on knowledge and intangible assets-based businesses:

BOX 3
The 'new' new economy –
a knowledge-based perspective

'The model of the *'new' New Economy* is based on an optimal combination of tangible and knowledge/ intangible assets – in the management focus is the ability to both create long-term value and short-term profits. In the 'new' New Economy, the main rules of the New Economy are still valid – such as that knowledge and intangible assets-based companies own more value-creation potential than tangible assets-based and traditional production companies. But at the same time some important rules of the old economy apply – that companies are in business to earn money. Therefore, in the new New Economy, businesses have to prove that their intangible strategy is paying off – through sustainable short-term profits – again and again. And at the same time, they have to show that they create long-term value through constant innovation, by increasing the value of their customer base through improved customer retention, by increasing the value of their human capital through constant skill build-up in their workforce, by increasing the value of their partner capital through new alliances and new forms of partnerships, and by increasing the value of their organisational capital through improved business processes and through organisational models that reflect the company's new business strategy and provide it with a competitive advantage.'

(*Source*: www.juergendaum.com/)

The knowledge economy is different from the new economy in a number of ways, not least the recognition of the importance of know-how, innovation, design and branding to the generation of a firm's competitive advantage and the social processes that create these.

Sources of competitive advantage in the knowledge economy

The knowledge economy does not consist exclusively of knowledge-intensive industries, but rather is characterised by new factors of production (WER, 2001) and new sources of competitive advantage, such as know-how, innovation, design and branding. The emphasis on know-how and innovation is supported by the work of a number of researchers and writers. Rees (2000) argues that a focus on innovation is essential for any analysis and understanding of the knowledge economy, and that a development strategy based on enhancing the innovative capacity of firms could be critical in improving economic performance. Nonaka and Takeuchi (1995) have developed a theoretical scheme that shows the important relational aspects between knowledge creation, continuous innovation and competitive advantage. Both of these arguments also find support in the work of Klein (2000), who focuses on product design and branding.

Product and service design and branding are vital elements in the knowledge-based economy, where 'the value of a business increasingly lurks not in physical and financial assets…but in intangible brands, patents, franchises, software, research programmes, ideas (and) expertise' (*The Economist*, 1999, p72). Therefore, as Browning and Reiss (2001) suggest, the creation and application of knowledge have transformed the *content* of production and consumption, and have

'...the knowledge economy will deepen the interdependence between the public and private sectors and between consumers and producers.'

thus affected the *nature* of the goods and services that are traded. This transformation goes further than the well-documented changes in the proportional and relative values of manufacturing versus service industries in the economy and demonstrates how the current transformation into a knowledge economy is very different in scale and character from that which has gone before.

Even where the product is manifestly physical (a pair of Nike trainers, for example), what is being produced and consumed goes beyond a pair of shoes to keep the feet warm and dry. It is also about the identity associated with the brand. The role of brands identified in Klein's (2000) analysis supports this argument. At the very least, consumers of fashion clothing with designer labels act as walking adverts for those labels. At a deeper level, though, there can be a symbiotic relationship between the identities of the consumer (fashion victim?) and the producer (brand exploiter?).

But it is not only the *content* of production and consumption that is changing and that defines the knowledge economy, it is also the *process* of production and consumption that is experiencing significant change. An interesting and important feature of the latter change is the nature of the relationships, and how they are conducted and mediated, between different economic actors.

Partnerships and collaborations in the knowledge economy

Leadbeater (2000) argues that the knowledge economy will deepen the interdependence between the public and private sectors and between consumers and producers. In the UK, the pursuit by the current government of public–private partnerships, and its co-operation with the financial sector in initiatives such as the People's

Bank, career development loans, and the now defunct individual learning accounts, are examples of the former interdependence. At the organisational level, we need only consider the new types of partnership between public-sector universities and private education providers in the e-learning arena. These 'e-university' collaborations operate both globally and nationally and are digital examples of public–private partnerships in the knowledge-based economy (see the Pricewaterhouse report on e-universities at www.hefce.ac.uk/pubs/hefce/2000/0044/00_44a1.doc).

Oxford University economist Alan Rugman makes a similar point in relation to multi-national corporations (MNCs). He defines MNCs as 'flagship' firms that operate at the hub of a business network. Members of their networks include key suppliers, key competitors, and what Rugman calls 'the non-business infrastructure' (Rugman, 2001, p16). This latter component of their network includes research and educational partners such as universities, and Rugman cites in-company executive development programmes as an example of their contribution. Rugman also emphasises the importance of tacit trust relationships as being at the heart of the partnerships that make up these networks.

Taking the firm as the next unit of analysis, there are significant developments in a company's interactions with its customers, suppliers, competitors and other organisations in its wider environment and the investment such organisations are willing to put into such relationships. Kaplan and Norton present several examples of a range of corporations seeking to 'improve asset utilisation through incorporating knowledge creation and exchange as part of their mission', resulting in 'a reduction in cash-to-cash cycles of investment in physical capital…in favour of investments in intellectual and human capital such as skilled technologists, databases, and customer-knowledgeable personnel' (1996, p59).

The specific nature of the communications between some of these economic actors is one that is increasingly supported by ICT. For example, customers of organisations such as Federal Express enter details of their requirements on-line, which then become the shipping control document. In terms of suppliers, business-to-business use of the Internet is growing in both volume and significance. The use of 'e-auctions' in the supply chain through industry trade networks such as World Wide Retail Exchange and dedicated operators such as Freemarkets.com are an illustration of both the changing relationships that firms can and do have with their suppliers, and of how those relationships are mediated.

Employees are not left out of these changing relationships. The WER (2001) suggests that, because of digital globalisation, companies are being compelled to rely on the creativity, current knowledge and the ability to acquire or create new knowledge of their core employees (see also Dixon, 2000). This has consequences that impact on the relationship between employers and employees, on the way work is organised, and on how learning for work is managed.

2 | Changes in the organisation of work

◰ **Concepts such as knowledge work and knowledge workers are now embedded in the lexicon of management practice.**

◰ **The change in the content and nature of work and the demand for skills is having an impact on the power relationship between managers and knowledge workers and is shifting the division of labour to a networked rather than hierarchical model.**

◰ **The knowledge creation process is increasingly dependent on collaborative working and social capital.**

◰ **The role of managers is moving away from a control orientation towards a more facilitating and enabling stance.**

◰ **A trend towards more flexible employment contracts is changing the way organisations support employees, influencing learning and career management.**

◰ **The growing demand for high-level skills influences approaches to work organisation, management practice and employment contracts.**

In the WER (2001) it is argued that the knowledge economy, and in particular the location-free nature of work, is transforming management practices, the employment contract and the quality of work. Bentley (1998) also suggests that in the knowledge economy, the division of labour is networked rather than hierarchical, and management practice is based on collaboration rather than command and control. These changes reflect two factors: the nature of knowledge and knowledge creation, and demand for skills in the changing work environment.

The influence of knowledge development on work organisation and relationships

The changing requirements for knowledge and the different processes of creating new knowledge are highly significant in bringing about changes in the organisation of work and the nature of the relationships between employers and employees. The notion of the 'knowledge-intensive firm' (KIF) is one that has been presented by academics for a number of years (Alvesson, 1993; 1995). The knowledge-intensive firm is taken to be one where most work is said to be of an intellectual nature, and where well-educated, qualified employees form the major part of the workforce. However, in the IPTS (2000) report it is argued that knowledge does not reside in organisations but rather that it is a function of inter-organisational activities – joint ventures and outsourcing, for example. As Leadbeater puts it, 'big companies in knowledge-intensive fields resemble a mother ship with a flotilla of smaller companies around it' (2000, p105). This point is supported when we consider the work of Pilemer and Racioppo (1999), who identified that some of the most successful companies use alliance-based strategies.

'...the composition of work teams will change more frequently, and so managers and other employees will need the ability to establish and de-establish relationships on a regular basis.'

Innovating is a knowledge creation process. Rugman's (2001) analysis suggests that innovation will increasingly depend on collaborative networks rather than on internal R&D departments. These will be both internal and external. Issues of confidentiality and competition are important here – to work, partnerships must be beneficial and unthreatening to all participants. Perhaps for this reason many private companies are teaming up with universities to solve problems – the focus is on complementarity, not competition. So employees will increasingly find themselves working in wide networks with others who are not part of their employing organisations. Their own continued employment, personal and career development, and working arrangements will be a function not only of their relationship with their direct employer but also of their relationships with the employees of collaborators in networks of employers.

In the previous chapter, two key influences were identified in relation to the creation of the knowledge economy, and their impact on both the *content* of products and services and the *process* of their production and consumption were examined. It will now be useful to sketch some similarly broad trends in the organisation of work and the implications of these trends for managerial and other roles.

The increasingly social nature of work organisation

The WER (2001) argues that gains in the performance of organisations operating in the knowledge economy will be a function of two related factors. The first is the application and exploitation of ICT. The authors argue, though, that this potential cannot be realised to the full without the second factor, which is a fundamental change in the way in which work is organised. In particular, the report identifies decentralised decision-making, the establishment of semi-autonomous teams and the use of project or task-oriented teams as necessary conditions. These features suggest a number of implications. First, the role of managers becomes less concerned with control and more focused on leadership. Second, the roles and jobs of employees become expanded in terms of responsibilities and accountabilities. Third, both managers and other employees are now required to be effective in working with others. Finally, the social context of work will be more transient; that is, the composition of work teams will change more frequently, and so managers and other employees will need the ability to establish and de-establish relationships on a regular basis.

The concept of social capital is useful here. Nahapiet and Ghoshal (1998) define social capital as 'the sum of actual and potential resources within, available through, and derived from the network of relationships possessed by an individual or social unit. Social capital thus comprises both the network and the assets that may be mobilised through the network' (p243). Without the abilities just described, then the trust and reciprocity necessary to add value through teams and networks will not be achieved. This perhaps adds weight to the view expressed in the Institute for Prospective Technological Studies report (2000) that interpersonal and social skills will be just as important to economic success as the technical skills associated with ICT.

The work of Field (2000) also suggests trends similar to those just discussed. According to his analysis, the role of managers is shifting to ensuring high quality in the output of work, from a previous concern with the efficiency of work processes. This view supports the WER findings in terms of employees having greater autonomy and discretion in decision-making, at least in terms of how they carry out their jobs. Employees with greater autonomy in the workplace may be more demanding of the kind and quality of the training and development they receive through work. The CIPD survey (2002) on who learns at work does show that higher-skilled workers are more likely to turn down training offered by their employers and to seek training independently outside the workplace. This supports the notion of the shift to the learner as a demanding consumer who wants a customised and high-quality learning experience. The move to greater autonomy for employees also supports a shift away from instruction-based modes of learning to those that focus more on learning facilitation and social learning.

A related trend identified by Field is that of a loosening of boundaries between jobs. This, in turn, is associated with a more general blurring of employment status, industries and economic sectors. Universities are an example of this blurring: are they part of the public or private sector? And if they are in the 'education industry', do their competitors include the private and corporate universities? Both of these are expanding their numbers. At the level of job roles, Field quotes the 1999 National Skills Task Force report conclusion that jobs are in fact losing clear occupational descriptors, and he goes on to provide the example of secretaries and the wider occurrence of multi-tasking to illustrate this trend. There are, though, some dangers, which are highlighted in the IPTS report (2000). It focuses in particular on the negative effects of work intensification. These effects include less time being spent on what the report describes as 'family, voluntary and community work and activities'. The concern expressed here echoes that

of Putnam (2000) in that such effects reduce the value of social capital.

A final general trend worth noting is that of growing flexibility in patterns of employment and work. This is well documented elsewhere and so need not be examined in detail here. However, increasing flexibility is of interest since it is arguably highly significant in creating some of the negative conditions surrounding changes in work organisation. This creates uncertainty and greater feelings of insecurity on the part of employees, which are added to by an emphasis on flexibility and tendencies to skill polarisation (see IPTS, 2000). A consequence of flexibilisation and the other trends mentioned here is that individuals need to be more willing and able to manage their own career (see also Knowles and Stewart, 2001). This requirement applies to all categories of employees, not just managers, and so can be said to be an impact with wider application (Field, 2000).

Knowledge firms, knowledge workers and knowledge management

As knowledge becomes the key focus of competitiveness and economic success, so a discourse arises with terms such as 'the knowledge firm', 'knowledge management', 'knowledge work' and 'knowledge workers' and new job titles emerge, such as 'Director of Intellectual Capital' (Boucher, 2001) and 'E-Working Change Manager' (Boucher, 2001). A useful starting point in examining the impact of the knowledge economy on the role of managers and other employers will be to describe the meaning of some of these terms, beginning with the concept of knowledge itself. Nonaka, Toyama and Konno adopt what they describe as the traditional definition of knowledge as 'justified true belief' (2002, p42).

They elaborate the definition by emphasising the dynamic, contextual and social nature of knowledge and its creation. They also usefully distinguish between two types of knowledge: explicit and tacit. Explicit knowledge can be directly expressed and communicated in the form of data, specifications and manuals, whereas tacit knowledge is personal and difficult to articulate. Nonaka and his colleagues suggest insights, intuitions and hunches as examples of tacit knowledge.

The distinction drawn between explicit or codified knowledge and tacit knowledge is important. This is important because explicit knowledge is tradable. That being the case, tacit knowledge, which by definition is not tradable, becomes crucial in sustaining and enhancing the competitive position of the firm. And there is a clear connection here with the concept of social capital. Networks based on trust and reciprocity are required for the creation and dissemination of tacit knowledge (see Field, 2000; Ecclestone and Field, 2001). The implication of this for the role of managers is that one of their primary tasks will be to build those networks both inside and outside their organisations.

The knowledge firm

Leadbeater (2000) suggests that knowledge creation requires organisations to adopt a number of characteristics:

◘ the holistic company securing public legitimacy

◘ entrepreneurial orientation

◘ fundamental innovators based on their ability to acquire specialist expertise and know-how

◘ cellular rather than hierarchical structure

◘ collaborative leadership

◘ self-managed employees with equitable pay and membership

◘ integration of diverse skills, different kinds of knowledge and complementary know-how.

He argues that 'creating a sense of enterprise is a vital job for corporate leadership' and that 'the cellular company needs to be underwritten by a social contract. Creating and maintaining that social contract is the job of senior managers' (Leadbeater, 2000, p85). This, then, suggests a new role for senior managers.

Knowledge workers

There are at the moment conflicting understandings of the term 'knowledge worker'. The WER (2001) presents knowledge workers as 'those who generate ideas and transmit them electronically as intangible or immaterial products', ICT providing such workers with access to the 'raw material' of knowledge creation. Scarbrough *et al* (1998, p10) report a view that with the increasing use of new technology, jobs across the occupational range are becoming more knowledge intensive and will therefore contain some element of 'knowledge work'.

However, linking knowledge creation only to the use of electronic media is highly restrictive. For example, therapists or HR consultants mainly impart their knowledge in a face-to-face situation, rather than via an electronic medium. Taking the argument one step further, all jobs (with or without electronic media use) have a knowledge component and can therefore be defined as

> **'Knowledge workers are demanding consumers of training, and often possess highly specialised knowledge that is at a level beyond that of the instructor or their own managers.'**

'knowledge work'. Field's (2000) analysis raises the additional problems of associating knowledge work with the service sector. As he points out, many service-sector roles remain in the category of 'McJobs' and so do not constitute knowledge work in the terms defined so far. Given these myriad perspectives, a clear definition is required. We suggest that the following from Scarbrough *et al* (1998) has both validity and utility:

Knowledge workers are characterised as individuals who have high levels of education and specialist skills combined with the ability to apply these skills to … identify and solve problems (Drucker, 1993). …Unlike earlier kinds of worker, knowledge workers now own the organisation's primary means of production ie knowledge – therefore the management of these workers assumes greater importance for retaining productivity than the management of machines, technologies or work processes. Knowledge workers are presented as a new type of occupation which is qualitatively different from the occupational groups of the old industrial economy. Their growing importance is associated with the emergence of a globalised, post-industrial economy in which knowledge displaces capital as the motor of competitive performance. (Scarbrough et al, 1998, p10.)

As noted earlier, the rise of the knowledge worker could have several implications for the training function. More flexible employment contracts change the way that companies and individuals view their training investment. Knowledge workers are demanding consumers of training, and often possess highly specialised knowledge that is at a level beyond that of the instructor or their own managers. They have much more control over what they learn and when they learn it, and are

unlikely to be coerced into training that they do not find relevant.

Knowledge management

Swan and Newell (1994) suggest that knowledge management (KM) relates to any process or practice that involves acquiring and using knowledge to enhance organisational performance. Moreover, KM processes are concerned with ensuring that once knowledge is acquired and used at one place and one time to solve a particular problem, it should be captured and shared so that the knowledge embedded in the solution can be reused at other places and times. KM is therefore obviously intimately related to issues of organisational learning (or the learning organisation), which is also about ensuring that learning accumulates over time within an organisation. The focus of KM is therefore to better leverage the intellectual capital that resides within organisational innovation processes.

Demand for new skills in the changing work environment

It is clear from the above discussion of knowledge and associated concepts that skills development and the management of learning in innovation processes will be a key role for all employees and their managers. The IPTS publication (IPTS, 2000) identifies growing demand for high-level skills in the EU. These skills relate in part to the technical skill associated with the application and exploitation of ICT, but other skills such as social, interpersonal and organisational are also identified as being important. Such skills are at a premium, not just because of the size of demand but also because they are critical to achieving economic success.

Their value, though, is also increased because of an ageing population and workforce and the consequent dependency ratio: the proportion of the population not in work relative to the proportion in work. Thus, in contrast to those with low skills, actual and potential employees holding such skills are in a position to demand and receive different approaches to the employment contract and management practices.

3 | Changes in organisational and individual learning

☒ **Learning achieved through and by social networks is an increasingly significant determinant of innovation and competitive advantage.**

☒ **Individuals and organisations are increasingly reliant on informal and workplace learning to provide necessary skills and future employability, but there are structural and cultural barriers that must be addressed to make workplace learning effective.**

☒ **Organisations are increasingly devolving responsibility for learning to managers and employees.**

☒ **Employees, however, show low levels of motivation to direct their own learning.**

☒ **Lack of attention and value attributed to learning by senior managers exacerbates the problem of low motivation to learn by employees.**

The important notion of social capital

The American sociologist Robert Putnam (1993) introduced the concept of social capital, and argued that social capital is the cause of both economic success and effective government. Social capital resides in the bonds of trust and reciprocity that are a feature of the relationships between networks of social and economic actors. Social capital, therefore, is an appropriate analytical tool in examining the implications for work organisation and the role of training and development in the knowledge economy. We shall have more to say about its meaning in the following sections of the report.

Organisational learning

The notion of organisational learning draws heavily upon the work of Argyris and Schon, especially their work on double-loop learning (Argyris and Schon, 1978). Recent writers, such as Dixon (1998), apply the well-known experiential

learning cycle (Kolb, 1984) to describing and explaining organisational learning processes. Both double-loop learning and experiential learning spotlight the natural learning that occurs through the everyday experience of work and organisational life, as opposed to formal and planned training and development processes. Such learning is an embedded part of knowledge creation and therefore of increasing significance in knowledge management. Its very embeddedness, though, means that it relies, in part, on the functioning of the workplace as a learning environment. Creating such environments is a key challenge for organisations in the knowledge economy.

Workplace learning

There are a number of terms that can be used interchangeably to refer to learning in and at work. These include: work-related, work-based and workplace learning. The CIPD (2000, p2) define workplace learning as those 'activities [that] include all the formal and non-formal training, instruction and coaching activities that go on, partly or wholly in the workplace'. It is clear that the CIPD's definition of workplace learning focuses on a mode of learning that is of increasing significance. This is confirmed by the CIPD's Training and Development Surveys, the latest of which shows an increase in the use of structured workplace learning (CIPD, 2001, p7). Further CIPD research shows that employees themselves also rely on this form of learning, particularly those with low skills (CIPD, 2002). There are, however, problems for organisations relying on this method of training and development.

Structural and cultural barriers to workplace learning

Both Rainbird (2000) and Sambrook (2001) report significant structural and cultural barriers to workplace learning, particularly in jobs that involve what has recently been described as 'emotional labour', as well as the traditional physical labour characteristic of the old economy. The term 'emotional labour' is taken to mean roles where employees are expected to conform to certain expectations about emotional display even when these conflict with their inner feelings (Taylor, 1998). When this conflict results in individuals suppressing genuine emotion or expressing fake emotion, the work or effort involved in doing so is termed 'emotional labour' (Mann, 1997). Emotional labour can have both functional and dysfunctional consequences for the individual and their organisations, is not necessarily confined to customer interactions, and is increasingly prevalent within all organisational communications.

While it is the case that emotional labour attracted the interest of academics in the past (Hochschild, 1983; Rafaili and Sutton, 1987; Van Maanen and

Kunda, 1989), it does not currently appear to be a major focus for either academics or managers. Nevertheless, the role of emotion in organisational life continues to be an important consideration (Fineman, 1993). Antonacopoulou and Gabriel (2001) related this to the learning process when they explored the extent to which emotions are products of learning, the ways in which emotions facilitate or inhibit learning, and the ways in which learning redefines and reorganises emotions at both an individual and an organisational level. Their analysis showed a clear interdependence between emotion and learning, and highlights many of the subtleties of individuals' reactions to change that current research into individuals' adaptability to organisational change tends to neglect.

Given the – perhaps not widely appreciated – importance of the nature of emotional labour and the place of emotion in the workplace, it will therefore be an important task for managers to identify how these barriers operate in their own context and to find ways of overcoming them that are relevant to that context. This is particularly important, given the general trend towards the devolution of responsibility for training and development away from the training function to line managers (Tjepkema et al, 2002; see also the next chapter).

Informal learning

Informal learning is that which is normally considered 'invisible', given that it is learning that occurs outside planned and explicit learning interventions. This invisibility leads to at least two problems. The first is controlling and exploiting this learning for the benefit of both the individual(s) and the organisation. The second is the difficulty of assessing and accrediting the results

> '...innovation requires both high levels of initial education
> and training on the part of employees and continuous
> individual and organisational learning.'

(Bjornavold, 2000). However, accentuating the positive, Rees (2000) emphasises the importance of informal and work-based learning to successful innovation (see also the CIPD report *The Future of Learning for Work*, Wilson *et al*, 2001).

Innovation and learning

Van de Ven (in Cooper and Argyris, 1998) defines an innovation as the creation and implementation of a new idea that might be technological (new technical artefacts, devices or products), a process (new services, programs or production procedures) or administrative (new institutional policies, structures or systems). He suggests that the idea may be a novel recombination of old ideas, a scheme that challenges the present order, or an unprecedented formula or approach; but as long as the idea is perceived as new and entails a novel change for those involved, it is an innovation.

There are direct connections between innovation and learning processes. As Rees (2000) argues, innovation requires both high levels of initial education and training on the part of employees and continuous individual and organisational learning. Rees's arguments find support in the work of Leadbeater, who argues that 'the locus of innovation is found in networks of learning' (2000, p132). These networks, which can be external or internal, are held together by relationships of social capital rather than structures or hierarchies (Nahapiet and Ghoshal, 1988), which, as Putnam and others (Coleman, 1998; Leana, 1999) recognise, require an ethic of trust and collaboration.

The implication of this for managers is that the employment relationship is now one that involves indirect rather than direct control. Indirect control 'involves "shaping" the organisational culture so that self-made (or team-made) decisions are in line with corporate needs and goals' (Watson, 1999) and employee empowerment and commitment are encouraged (Legge, 1995) by their inclusion in decisions about their daily activities. This requires 'facilitating the continuous development of employees and their knowledge (Watson, 1999, p30). These views add even more credence to the notion that managing learning will be a key task for both managers and non-managerial employees (Tjepkema *et al*, 2002).

This will represent a challenge, since the work of both Tjepkema *et al* (2002) and the IPTS (2000) identify low levels of self-motivation for learning on the part of organisational members across Europe. Low levels of motivation on the part of employees are not helped by a lack of attention and value attribution by senior managers (Field, 2000). A CIPD research report (Miller, Rankin and Neathey 2001) on competency frameworks in UK organisations, for example, shows that only around half of those organisations surveyed include a competency relating to the development of others in their management competency frameworks. Organisations will clearly need to put more emphasis on the importance of employee development if managers are to begin to take this part of their role seriously.

This chapter has highlighted the links between changes at a global level and changes in the nature and focus of organising and managing work in the knowledge economy. It has also drawn attention to the importance of organisational and individual learning for competitive success. However, it is clear from the analysis that individual employees are increasingly required to manage their own continuing learning, and to rely on the workplace itself as a site and source of learning. We move in the next chapter to examine the implications of this trend.

4 | The impact of changes on employee training and development

◪ **Employee retention is vital for organisations in the knowledge economy. Development opportunities will play a key role in the recruitment and retention strategies of knowledge-based organisations.**

◪ **A greater variety of approaches to training delivery, including informal and workplace learning, coaching, communities of practice and the use of e-learning, are becoming more widely used.**

◪ **Individual employees are increasingly expected to be responsible for, and active in, their own learning and development.**

◪ **Individual employees can respond negatively to their new responsibility and new approaches, including e-learning.**

◪ **'Blended learning', which combines e-learning and non-ICT approaches, may often be more effective than solutions based solely on e-learning.**

◪ **The use of corporate universities to manage organisational and individual learning, and to provide a mechanism for creating internal and external learning networks, is increasing.**

As we have seen so far, the knowledge economy is presented in the literature as resulting from globalisation and the increasing digitalisation of social and economic life with the widespread use of information and communication technologies (ICT). In this context, although knowledge has always been viewed as an organisational asset, it is now being explored more in the literature and is more widely recognised in organisational practice, with organisations seen as knowledge systems. Amongst academics, this knowledge-based view of organisations is examined in a variety of disciplinary areas, including information systems management, strategic management, organisation theory, marketing, entrepreneurship, accounting, and strands of sociology, psychology, economics, and philosophy (Scarbrough *et al*, 1998).

In business studies, the organisation is presented as consisting of bundles of knowledge assets that require effective management in order to gain competitive advantage. Part of this management process must now include a consideration of the relationship between the management of knowledge assets and the processes of learning. There are a number of reasons the management of learning must occur in parallel with the management of knowledge.

Impact of environmental changes on learner behaviour
Learning and retention

The general focus on managers supporting the learning and development of their staff is

> '...the knowledge of key employees is directly related to the core competencies of the organisation, which in turn represent knowledge assets...'

important, not least in the specific case of employee retention, since provision of, and opportunities for, development (both personal and career-related) has long been recognised as important in employee retention (Harrison, 2000). In the context of the knowledge economy, employee retention is vital for two reasons. First, the knowledge of key employees is directly related to the core competencies of the organisation, which in turn represent knowledge assets (Nonaka and Nishiguchi, 2002, p55). Second, and relatedly, these assets depend not only on the development of tacit knowledge over time, but also on the trust relationships developed between employees and management (WER, 2001).

Social learning and communities of practice

Roles have also changed because of the tendency towards flatter and more decentralised organisations; the widespread adoption of information technology to support 'virtual' forms; the diffusion of team arrangements (CIPD, 1999); the increasing volatility and *ad hoc* character of co-ordination structures; and the increasing reliance on networks of alliances (www.spbo.unibo.it/kio/proposal.htm).

Included in these networks of alliances are what have become known as communities of practice. Communities of practice consist of networks of people who work together in an organisation and who regularly share information and knowledge. Such people may be, but are not necessarily, part of formal teams or units. They often collaborate on particular projects or products, or they hold the same or similar jobs. They have been described as 'peers in the execution of real work'. Communities of practice are held together by shared goals and a need to learn from each other (Seely Brown and Solomon Gray, 1997). It can be argued that

deliberately developing learning processes that reflect these principles can enable managers to meet both their formal responsibility for encouraging learning at work *and* any inherent orientation they may have to develop their staff.

Coaching and mentoring

Perhaps because of flatter organisational structures and the growing power of knowledge workers, there has been an increase in demand for coaching and mentoring. This fits in with the idea of a shift away from instruction-based methods of learning to one that focuses on providing support as individuals address problems and challenges for themselves. It is also in line with the CIPD research findings that indicate learning from colleagues and peers is a favourite method of learning among employees (CIPD, 2002). Coaching can occur in this way, colleagues helping each other to learn new skills and resolve technical or organisational problems. Alternatively, managers can coach individuals by helping them to understand the expectations of higher managers and give support in taking on more difficult responsibilities. But coaching and mentoring can also be a more formal arrangement, with a specific coach or mentor assigned to an individual. The aim is not to instruct but to support the individual, share experience, and give advice.

Knowledge management (KM) and continuous professional development

The knowledge economy and the advent of the knowledge-based organisation require particular responses from training specialists operating in different sectors. However, as reported in Scarbrough *et al* (1998), personnel management professionals generally are not taking up the issue and ownership of KM, being usurped in this by others such as information systems (IS) professionals 'who have done so in part because they see it as an opportunity to influence corporate strategy and to raise the profile and status of IS' (Scarbrough *et al*, 1998, p44). Furthermore, in spite of this increased coverage, it is debatable the extent to which training and personnel practitioners have managed to 'get a lever' on issues of knowledge management to any great degree (Benson, 1997 in Scarbrough *et al*, 1998, p43).

Learner motivation

Another important consideration is that of learner motivation. Recent research has shown that there are connections between the notions of informal learning and self-managed learning, suggesting that where organisations seek to encourage the former they also seek to encourage the latter, and vice versa. So employees are increasingly required to accept responsibility for managing their own learning and development, and to use less formal and work-based methods in doing so. Evidence suggests, however, that employees are not motivated enough to manage this process effectively (Tjepkema *et al*, 2002). The notion of communities of practice, described earlier, is one way in which less formal routes to learning may be

encouraged. Significantly, however, individual employees may or may not be motivated actually to engage in those processes.

The impact of technology on training

Training cannot ignore the impact of ICT. This applies to both training delivery and the training needs created by the application of ICT in business operations. The latest CIPD Annual Training Survey (CIPD, 2001) shows that the use of a wide range of technology continues to rise (see Figure 3). Research conducted for the DTI in 2000 (www.employment-studies.co.uk, 2001) identified retail sector skills needs arising from the application of ICT in electronic retailing. The results categorised those needs under four headings:

◘ Management skills – these included project, logistics, supply chain and contracting/ partnership management skills

◘ Technical skills – these refer to ICT-specific skills and encompass what the report refers to as 'skills in depth' (eg computer languages, database construction and interactive design), 'skills in breadth' (forging links with other elements of the retailer's systems to provide

Figure 3 | Net changes in the use of technological training methods, 1999–2001*

* Net changes in the percentage of respondents who use these methods

(*Source*: CIPD, 2001)

> **'A widely accepted definition of e-learning is…"learning that is delivered, enabled or mediated by electronic technology for the explicit purpose of training in organisations."**

and maintain integrated solutions) and 'context' (understanding retailing and their particular organisation).

◘ Other technical skills – online marketing skills (eg exploiting the customer information) and customer service skills (particularly the 'fulfilment' end).

◘ Generic skills (skills applying at all points of the business, eg corporate entrepreneurship and increased levels of understanding about ICT and its potential).

This four-part model could be applied to many sectors.

E-learning

As well as having a significant impact on ways of doing business, the growth in applications of ICT has the potential to provide new alternatives for the professional practice of training and development. While the prefix 'e' can be and is applied to almost any word, the term 'e-learning' has achieved some currency. A widely accepted definition of e-learning is that which is provided by the CIPD as 'learning that is delivered, enabled or mediated by electronic technology for the explicit purpose of training in organisations. It does not include stand-alone technology-based training such as the use of CD-ROMs in isolation' (www.cipd.co.uk).

In spite of expectations to the contrary, 'the market for e-learning has been slow to take off' (*The Economist*, 17 February 2001, p101). One reason for this may be that the term is commonly applied to only one particular application of ICT in training and development practice, and that is the provision of new and alternative delivery channels.

Other elements and activities in that practice receive less attention in much of the writing on the subject.

Perhaps one of the reasons for this is that those who are currently training are continuing in the traditional training 'modes', and e-learning is being developed by 'newcomers'. Smidt (1999) argues that new ICT media will tend to recruit 'pioneers' attracted by a new medium. This creates two 'knowledge communities', which has the danger of splitting the provision of training into two distinct approaches: the extensive use of e-learning that might not take account of lessons learned about training pedagogy and delivery, and the continuation of standard face-to-face training that does not take account of new demands by learners for the supply of flexible communications technologies.

Learners and e-learning

It has been argued that e-learning is not a popular choice of learning medium for learners (Field, 2000, p97), and this point has been reinforced in other research surveys such as the CIPD survey *Who Learns at Work?* (CIPD, 2002). For example, the MORI (1998) survey *Attitudes to Learning* reported that learners had a preference for books, other written materials and lectures. However, the pace of technology is so fast that learners at the time of the MORI survey may not have had much (if any) experience of e-learning and could therefore not make a meaningful judgement on what an e-learning experience consisted of and whether they would prefer to use ICT to learn. Given the findings in the CIPD Training Survey Report (CIPD, 2001) that show that 16.5 per cent of those surveyed use e-learning regularly and there are expectations for major growth, we shall soon have a clearer picture of how people interact with this mode of learning delivery.

For those actually engaged in the e-learning experience, there are a number of factors that trainers need to take into account with regard to e-learners' experiences (Sloman, 2001a). Research conducted by Sambrook (2001) identifies factors that learners find influence their responses to the use of e-learning. These are categorised into a hierarchy of three levels: those to do with the learning process itself, those to do with use of learning materials (whether computer-based or not) and those specifically to do with computer-based learning materials. Influencing factors in each of these levels are further categorised in terms of the chronological order of the learning experience, labelled as 'getting in, getting on and getting out'. The resulting framework is given in Table 1.

Training specialists need to address these factors in the design and delivery of e-learning, keeping

constantly updated on the challenges of this form of training (see webpages such as Elliott Masie's www.learningdecisions.com or www.masie.com, for example). Sambrook's research suggests that the factors are not in themselves necessarily positive or negative: they can work in either or both directions for different individual learners, depending upon context and circumstances. The task of the trainer, therefore, is to understand the operation of these factors in those contexts and circumstances, and to minimise negative and maximise positive effects (Sloman, 2001a).

A number of additional questions arise when we consider the implementation of e-learning:

◘ What is happening in e-learning in other countries that we can benchmark? (Sloman, 2001b)

Table 1 | Factors influencing learning: hierarchical themes

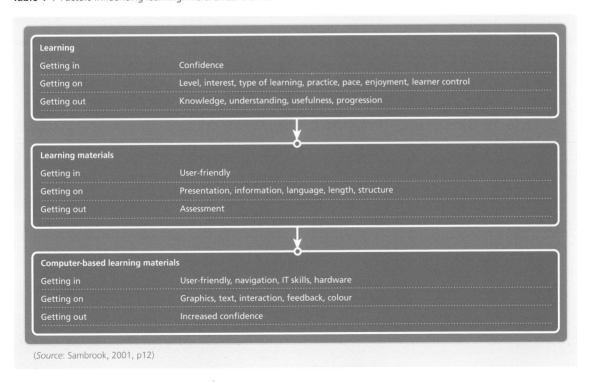

Learning	
Getting in	Confidence
Getting on	Level, interest, type of learning, practice, pace, enjoyment, learner control
Getting out	Knowledge, understanding, usefulness, progression

Learning materials	
Getting in	User-friendly
Getting on	Presentation, information, language, length, structure
Getting out	Assessment

Computer-based learning materials	
Getting in	User-friendly, navigation, IT skills, hardware
Getting on	Graphics, text, interaction, feedback, colour
Getting out	Increased confidence

(*Source*: Sambrook, 2001, p12)

◘ Which combination of emerging learning technologies should be selected?

◘ What needs to take place for planning for use of the Internet to support professional learning? (Senior, 2001)

◘ To what extent should dedicated physical facilities be replaced by virtual networks, or formal instruction by shared learning within the work process?

◘ How can employees be taught how to use technologies like the Internet for their learning? (Senior, 2001)

◘ Are there particular learning styles for e-learning? (see www.cipd.co.uk/Infosource/ Training/Learningstylesine-learning.asp)

◘ How and what might be the impact of e-learning on training evaluation?

◘ In e-learning environments, how might training specialists justify their personal and collective contributions?

Blended solutions

In addition to the myriad of questions that can be applied to e-learning, one key theme is emerging from the debate – the concept of blended solutions. Zenger and Uehlein (2001) argue that a truly blended solution has the following characteristics:

◘ *a completely integrated instructional design* with a consistent framework and nomenclature – e-learning elements are not just 'bolted on' to disparate elements of traditional training

practice and training delivery, but coherently integrated and amalgamated according to training needs

◘ *each method delivering its best*, which means 'that e-learning delivers content and handles the learning management processes, process assessments and feedback tools. It delivers content and robust simulations that must come over the Web. The instructor-led sessions are used for content that requires touching people's emotions, for practice and rehearsal, for discussion of the challenges participants will face implementing what they've learned back on the job, and for feedback between participants.'

◘ *maximum flexibility*, where 'learners benefit in situations in which more than one delivery method can successfully accomplish a learning objective: learners can choose which to use. Some people prefer content delivered in a discovery or experiential way, others prefer linear, deductive content. Blended solutions provide options.'

◘ *variety*, where 'learning approaches include assessments, online coaching and mentoring, self-paced Web-delivered content, behaviour modelling, simulations, full-motion video and online testing'.

Zenger and Uehlein (2001, p58) also suggest that a number of constraints exist on the implementation of blended learning solutions in organisations:

◘ Training specialist competence tends to exist either in instructor-led training or e-learning, but seldom both.

◘ Major front-end investment is required for e-learning, which invariably demands a large population of learners in order to justify the investment, which in turn means the content selected for delivery must be widely applicable, in contrast to highly specialised content related to a small aspect of one job.

◘ Despite actual e-learning *delivery* being relatively inexpensive, the costs are higher for the instructional *design and skills* required to combine instructor-led learning with technology-delivered learning.

◘ Resistance to something new by those responsible for the training provision in organisations and other possible stakeholders, such as line managers, employees, suppliers and customers.

The surveys regularly conducted by CEDEFOP (see http://lists.trainingvillage.gr/lists/etv-newsletter/) support many of these points. It can be seen, then, that in the tendency to consider the 'e' aspect of e-learning there is a danger that the learning and provision of blended training solutions might be forgotten.

The corporate university

ICT has also encouraged the development of the corporate university, a notion that organisations across the world are adopting as the defining mechanism for structuring their training and development function (Meister, 1998). The corporate university is currently the fastest-growing form of university, but many misunderstand its nature and purpose when they suggest that companies invest in establishing and developing a corporate university in order to provide employees with the opportunity to study for a degree.

The actual wider purpose and role of corporate universities is illustrated by Phillips (1999) who emphasises first that the concept refers to a process rather than a place, second that the customer base encompasses suppliers and customers as well as all levels of employees, and third that the focus is any or all learning relevant to enhanced job or role performance and, finally, that improved business performance is the main rationale for investment in a corporate university. Phillips' final point finds support among many other writers (see Barnett, 2000, for example).

Field also notes the growth of corporate universities and reports an estimate of 1,200 being in existence worldwide in 1999 (2000, p79). He also comments on the debate surrounding the potential threat to established and traditional universities. As with others (eg Prince and Stewart, under review), Field suggests that the future is more likely to see a growth of collaborative partnerships between the two forms of university rather than the newer form replacing the older form. This is partly linked to the role of corporate universities in the attempts by companies to become learning organisations (see Miller and Stewart, 1999).

Such collaborations may also be seen as attempts to overcome the much-vaunted academic–vocational divide (Crick, 2000). They may also be the results of an increasing recognition that organisational learning requires co-operation and networking with those outside the organisation and especially with knowledge-creating institutions such as universities (Daniel, 1999; Rees, 2000). What is clear is that collaborative relationships between corporate and traditional universities provide the prospect of building the social capital of both and, in the case of the former, of training and development functions.

'In structural terms, establishing a corporate university
is one mechanism for co-ordinating and exploiting
organisational learning processes and their outcomes.'

In structural terms, establishing a corporate university is one mechanism for co-ordinating and exploiting organisational learning processes and their outcomes. In this sense, and as Prince and Stewart (under review) argue, corporate universities are a clear contribution to knowledge management strategies from the training and development function. This is achieved in part from the direct involvement of managers and employees from all levels and all functions of the business in the strategic and operational activities of the corporate university. It is also achieved by corporate universities, in partnership with IT/IS departments, leading in the utilisation of ICT for corporate learning and knowledge management. These two features are present in the business/ operating models adopted by both Unipart and Lloyds TSB for their UK-based corporate universities.

BOX 4

The University for Lloyds TSB (UfLTSB)

The UfLTSB was launched in July 1999 as a corporate university created solely for the benefit of Lloyds TSB Group staff. Established following a merger of Lloyds Bank and the TSB Group, the UfLTSB was strongly influenced by government policy on learning as outlined in the White Paper *The Learning Age*. The main objectives of the UfLTSB are:

- to make learning more accessible to staff within the group, when and where the learner needs it

- to ensure a closer link between learning available and the needs of the business.

The UfLTSB offers both 'virtual' and 'real' learning opportunities to staff. It has so far established a network of 2,000 Multimedia PCs (MMPCs), which means that for most the opportunity to access learning should be no more than 10 minutes' travelling time away. In addition, staff can access and obtain details of learning opportunities on the Intranet and Internet.

According to Lloyds TSB, what makes their corporate university distinctive is that it pulls learning and development together under one roof so there is a consistent approach in line with business need. The governance structure of UfLTSB plays an important role in this approach. The establishment of a governing 'strategy board', comprising some of the group's most senior directors and chaired by the group director of HR, has been instrumental in securing a high level of support across the group. The role of the strategy board is to make sure that the UfLTSB curriculum meets the strategic needs of the business. To this end, critical areas of the business are represented as 'faculties' within the UfLTSB; each faculty is headed by a business unit director who is a member of the strategy board. There are seven faculties, as follows:

- Faculty of Management

- Faculty of Customer Service

- Faculty of Sales

- Faculty of Operations

- Faculty of Change

- Faculty of Risk

- Faculty of Information Technology.

5 | Lessons for the future of the training and development profession

☒ **The training function plays a key role in creating competitive advantage in the knowledge economy.**

☒ **The notion of 'social capital' will be significant in achieving that contribution.**

☒ **Training specialists will need to adopt new roles to achieve their contribution.**

☒ **Supporting informal learning within organisations will be a key role for training professionals.**

☒ **Trainers will be increasingly expected to create more complex blends of learning approaches and delivery mechanisms to deliver customised results.**

☒ **Helping managers to understand and carry out new responsibilities for supporting learning and motivating learners will be an important function of the training role.**

☒ **A key shift in role is from training provider to learning facilitator and internal consultant.**

☒ **Training specialists will need to respond to organisational and individual training needs arising from implementation of knowledge management strategies.**

In this chapter we consider the implications for the training function of taking a knowledge-based view of organisations. We specifically explore the changes that may be necessary for the strategic and operational focus of training and development provision in relation to employees. The areas under consideration are the:

☒ strategic focus of training and development provision

☒ role of the training function

☒ structure of the training function

☒ content of training programmes

☒ training of professional staff

☒ impact of technology on training

☒ state of training in the SME environment.

> 'Incorporating a knowledge-based view of the organisation requires an organisational strategy for a knowledge management (KM) approach.'

Strategic focus of training and development provision

Incorporating a knowledge-based view of the organisation requires an organisational strategy for a knowledge management (KM) approach. Blake suggests that, as a collection of methods for harnessing corporate knowledge, 'KM is the process of capturing a company's collective expertise wherever it resides and distributing it to wherever it can help produce the biggest payoffs' (Blake, 1998 in Scarbrough et al, 1998). KM is therefore an important activity, the implementation of which has an impact on organisational cultures, structures and technologies. Because KM encompasses processes that seek synergistic combinations of data and information-processing systems, *and the creative and innovative capacity of human beings* (Malhotra, 2000, our emphasis), then the training function has a vital role in creating these synergies. Scarbrough et al (1998) go so far as to suggest that rather than being seen in terms of skill formation, training and development would better be viewed as knowledge creation and utilisation.

But all of this requires a serious change of perspective, strategy and operations by those managing and delivering training. In addition to attempting this changed perspective, the training function also needs to be geared up to support KM initiatives, with any training interventions clearly linked to organisational, IT, HRM and HRD strategies and organisational learning processes. When the organisation is operating transnationally, there is also a need for training strategies to have regard for both institutional and cross-cultural aspects of managerial knowledge transfer and managerial and organisational learning.

The adoption and implementation of ICTs within organisations requires extensive investment of financial and other resources and involves complex activity processes, especially when those ICTs are organisation-wide and integrated, such as enterprise resource planning (ERP) systems. In Box 5 (opposite) we extract important key definitions from the research of Newell et al (2001), who examined a particular aspect of the development of ERP systems in a transnational organisation.

Newell et al's (2001) research reinforces the view that, as networks become increasingly important to organisational life, so will social capital. Social capital, therefore, provides a very useful concept to be applied in devising training and development contributions that cohere with organisational strategies. For example, development interventions around team development and team working can facilitate the building of relationships congruent with increasing the value and extent of existing social capital. In addition, and as Newell et al (2001) also showed in their case study, negative social capital can be an inhibitor to the achievement of organisational objectives.

Ecclestone and Field (2001) examine the application of the concept of social capital within the context and practice of vocational education and training. They report their conclusions on the positive and negative outcomes of the operation of networks with the high levels of trust and reciprocity associated with positive social capital. Their conclusions are based on a review of a number of research projects, including several focused on skill formation and the acquisition of skills and knowledge exchange among adults. The positive outcomes of promoting social capital are that its existence:

- overcomes the 'prisoners' dilemma': in other words, members of the networks operate in a 'win–win' fashion

- reduces the costs of job search: because networks act as informal recruitment agencies and so reduce costs for both prospective employers and employees

- lowers the risks associated with innovation: this is a function of high levels of trust and the spread of risk

- promotes flows of information: of particular importance here is the sharing/dissemination of tacit knowledge and embedded skills

- supports schools in promoting human capital: the networks studied encourage school-age children to gain qualifications

- combats 'free riding': this applies to the practice of poaching by employers and that of 'freeloading' by employees.

BOX 5

Enterprise resource planning in a transnational organisation

ERP systems are based on developing a common IT infrastructure and common business processes, and provide a means of integrating core corporate activities of an enterprise, such as finance, logistics and human resources. They provide for the identification of the organisation's resources and the application of them in the most effective manner to fulfil the business objectives. Developed in response to the need to manage across global businesses (which is difficult when each business is using different systems and technologies), ERP is therefore claimed to be a business solution implemented to support the integration of business activity.

Knowledge management in ERP project teams: In ERP project teams each individual member not only has unique knowledge, skills and expertise which can be drawn upon during the design and implementation of an ERP system, but also a unique network which might therefore broaden the reach of the project team across the potential user community. This knowledge is dispersed both within the organisation (eg across functional groups and between hierarchical levels) and across organisations (eg with consultants, software suppliers, other firms) (Hislop et al, 1997). The

successful completion of these project tasks will depend on selecting project team members with appropriate knowledge, skills and expertise, so project teams ideally will be chosen so that their members have a mix of knowledge and capabilities (Grandori and Soda, 1995). It is unlikely, however, that project team members will have all the relevant knowledge and expertise necessary, either to design the system *per se* or to ensure that it is accepted and implemented by all those for whom it is intended.

Learning, training and the generation of social capital by ERP project team members: As well as receiving formal training in systems development work, project team members network with a range of other individuals in order to appropriate the necessary knowledge and gain commitment from those who will use the system. In this they will draw upon their collective social capital, defined by Nahapiet and Ghoshal (1998) as 'the sum of actual and potential resources within, available through, and derived from the network of relationships possessed by an individual or social unit. Social capital thus comprises both the network and the assets that may be mobilised through the network' (p243).

> '...training specialists must take into account the important role that the generation of social capital plays in organisational practice when developing training strategies and interventions.'

Some of these positive outcomes in relation to processes of skills acquisition and knowledge exchange find their antithesis in the negative outcomes listed below.

Social capital:

◘ promotes inefficient and ineffective recruitment and selection; in other words, there is no necessary match between the abilities of recruits and job requirements

◘ condones insider trading; this is an example of social capital being used for 'bad' rather than 'good' ends

◘ within networks, places low value on formalised knowledge and certificated skills; this is not necessarily the case but it can be found in many employment contexts

◘ inhibits free flow of information between networks; the cohesion of a particular network can act as a barrier to interaction with other networks

◘ encourages networks to be slow to change and resistant to policy interventions; this point is similar to the previous outcomes but the particular focus here is deliberate attempts through policy interventions to bring about change.

Notwithstanding the findings of the potential negative outcomes of social capital by researchers such as Newell *et al* (2001) and Ecclestone and Field (2001), it is clear that training specialists must take into account the important role that the generation of social capital plays in organisational practice when developing training strategies and interventions. This is because without such

interventions negative outcomes can so easily be associated with negative values of social capital and a lack of congruence with organisational objectives.

The changing role of the training function

As noted in previous paragraphs, a key role of the training function in the future will be in the support of knowledge management initiatives and social capital construction. Training specialists need to be involved in disseminating the message throughout the organisation that attempts to manage organisational knowledge must be founded on an understanding of how people learn, how they implement what they learn, and how they share their knowledge.

Given that this will involve working with social networks, perhaps in the form of work teams and irregularly constituted project teams, it therefore follows that training specialists will become much more focused on informal rather than formal learning processes. And given that 'successful companies will engage the intelligence of their consumers to improve their products' (Leadbeater, 2000, p33), the client base of the training function will be much wider than previously. This new role of 'non-employee development' (Harrison, 2000) will therefore become much more important.

The building of social capital, a widening client base and the support of knowledge management all imply a shift from the role of *training provider* to one of *learning facilitator*. This in turn suggests a need for the adoption of new teaching methodologies in fulfilling the new role of the training function. The WER (2001) supports this view and it also argues that there is a need for a primary focus on the process of learning rather than the content. In other words, *how* training and development are delivered becomes more important than *what* is delivered. This follows from the view that 'the ability to learn is a source of competitive advantage' (p10). Training processes rather than content, then, are more significant in developing the ability to learn, and should therefore be the primary focus. The WER (2001) also highlights the significance and importance of daily learning in the job, which further reinforces this changing role of the training specialist in supporting informal rather than formal learning.

The points made so far are supported by empirical evidence from recent research across Europe, which also points to additional changes in the role of training (Tjepkema *et al*, 2002). These include a more strategic contribution through more regular and closer contact with senior decision-makers and a role as internal consultant in relation to operational managers and employees. Closer contact enables and supports training specialists in their efforts to facilitate informal learning, and in the application of newer methodologies such as coaching and mentoring, which in turn helps employees to develop their learning abilities and skills. The research also noted changes in structural relationships to support the achievement of these new roles.

Training has traditionally been located as part of personnel in organisational structures. More recent trends would suggest that training is increasingly recognised as vital to KM and therefore new structural relationships are being adopted.

The development needs of trainers in the new economy

Based on our review of the literature, there is little currently known about the training and

development needs of training specialists associated with the knowledge economy. This may in part explain why Tjepkema *et al* (2002) found hardly any mention in their study of 28 companies of the development of training staff as part of measures to respond to changing organisational strategies. We therefore have little empirical evidence to report on this subject.

Our analysis so far does, however, suggest that development needs will arise from the new roles of training specialists. These will include, for example:

- e-moderator

- learning facilitator

- strategic partner

- internal consultant

- network co-ordinator.

Fulfilling these roles will require specialists to have an in-depth understanding of the nature of the knowledge economy, as well as of the particular applications of ICT in training practice. Related to this, they will require knowledge and understanding of advances in learning theories, especially those associated with learning as a social process, so that they can facilitate group and organisational as well as individual learning. Application of the concept of social capital theory will also be important. The ability to apply methods and techniques relevant to non-employee development is also relevant here. Additional items related to the training needs of training specialists include the following:

- maintaining a high level of specialist knowledge, not only in training and development, but also in business strategy and practice

◘ maintaining awareness of changing employment structures for themselves and their clients

◘ becoming reflective practitioners in the way they encourage their clients to do (Schon, 1987).

How training specialists attempt to meet their needs could include the following methods:

◘ gaining knowledge about the services and support available for trainers via their professional body to help their varied learning requirements and to support their needs for relevant professional information, knowledge and contacts

◘ being prepared to respond to high job demands and address difficulties in managing their CPD

◘ expending effort on using the Internet to support their CPD

◘ forming networks, partnerships or discussion groups, whether virtual or otherwise, in order to provide both employed and self-employed training professionals with informal learning opportunities.

Trainers need to be able to continually investigate what is happening externally in training and development, particularly e-learning aspects, in order to benchmark their own practice. The development of e-learning is of major importance for training and education, but information about its scale, rate of growth and the areas of training

in which it is having an impact is inadequate. There is a need to maintain a knowledge base of meaningful information, which can be gained from a variety of sources. These include membership of e-mailing lists of training networking groups such as The Training Village (http://lists.trainingvillage.gr/lists/etv-newsletter/2000/index.html), referred to in the previous section, and the CIPD's webpage discussion area (www.cipd.co.uk/elearning/Board/e-learning/window.asp). Alternatively, information pages such as those offered by the European Commission on issues such as insights about the state of e-learning in Europe (http://europa.eu.int/comm/education/elearning/what.htm) are equally valuable.

Finally, the skills identified in the DTI research mentioned earlier will also apply to training specialists. At the very least, the generic skills suggested in that research will be relevant, and the management skills will also apply to those training specialists with management responsibilities. More specifically, trainers will need to design and deliver training programmes for knowledge management.

The content of training programmes

There is a requirement for trainers to provide courses where the content is highly specific to organisational need. These should be developed to incorporate an assessment of employees' current knowledge and skills and a clarification of training priorities to enable people to improve their organisational contribution. Where transnational organisations or cross-cultural collaborations are involved, then training materials need to be adapted to reflect local industrial context and experience, and care needs to be taken that the Western version of the knowledge-based enterprise is not incorrectly dominant in training sessions.

'**If there is a strategy in the organisation for an emerging cultural convergence, then this needs to be taken into account in training too...**'

Forethought needs to be given to deriving an appropriate corporate culture reflecting the geographical area, and trainers need to transcend personal cultural bias when designing and/or delivering training. Furthermore, these issues need to be addressed in the inter-cultural training experience. If there is a strategy in the organisation for an emerging cultural convergence, then this needs to be taken into account in training too.

Training for professional staff

Barrie and Pace (1997) consider the area of professional staff and attempt to link competencies, efficiency and organisational learning. They suggest that those responsible for training need to take into consideration a number of issues. For example, they argue that:

◘ training for competitiveness is more a function of improving the technical and social learning processes than a function of improving technical performance alone

◘ the focus for learning needs to be on maximising training opportunities in the workplace, rather than on off-the-job courses

◘ professionals working in multi-disciplinary teams need to be trained how to gain information about knowledge and expertise outside their own specialism

◘ the demands for new knowledge and expertise is high, requiring a 'just-in-time' approach to much training

◘ the Internet is providing opportunities and challenges both for gaining a wide range of information and for accessing new learning opportunities, often through sharing of

experiences. Greater consideration therefore needs to be taken of the role of the Internet in training, because it is having a major effect on the way professionals work, with increased communication with people both within and outside their employing organisation.

◘ there must be efforts to maintain knowledge about the significant developments by other organisations in the design and generation of websites to meet learners' changing requirements

◘ because professional careers in particular have become more uncertain and less structured, requiring individuals not only to move between employers but also to work across traditional professional boundaries, then training for professionals needs to contribute both to enhanced career opportunities and to business performance, and greater support is needed for professionals throughout their careers (ie via mentoring) in order to share and network with other professionals

◘ professional staff can have a major influence on attitudes to and support for learning in the workplace, especially in SMEs.

Training for knowledge management

With the growing understanding that the identification and effective use of employee and organisational knowledge is a distinct competitive advantage, locating core knowledge in organisations is a vital activity. This is a complex task involving a number of aspects, and the training function has a key role in facilitating learning and action in this area. Training courses therefore need to be developed that cover the full range of the knowledge management process.

Some training providers supply materials and guides for knowledge management training. These webpages carry valuable information that can be taken into account when devising strategies for training in the area of knowledge management, and a glance at the content can show how seriously the training provider has considered the integrative nature of the training they are offering (see, for example, Fenman Ltd at www.fenman.co.uk/).

Particular areas to question can be seen in Box 6 (opposite).

In planning for the provision of appropriate training programmes in the organisation operating in the knowledge-based economy, a number of issues have been addressed, such as: the nature of the strategic focus of training and development provision, the changing role and structure of the training function, the nature of the content of training programmes and the impact of technology on training. In considering these issues, however, a number of other issues need to be highlighted for further consideration, including:

- How can training address the trend for a balance of individual and corporate interests? (Coulson-Thomas, 1999)

- How might training address the tension between supplying support (on the one hand) to downsizing, cost-cutting and re-engineering activities and (on the other) to revenue generation and value creation activities such as knowledge management? (Bassi, 1997)

- What new competencies will be required to support knowledge management initiatives?

- How can an employee's or team's skill, knowledge and learning be transferred from one part of the organisation to another? (Lank, 1998)

- What should be the balance between formal and informal learning? (Coulson-Thomas, 1999)

- To what extent should training and development activities be outsourced?

- Which of the collaborative or partnership relationships on offer should be entered into?

- How do we take account of the different set of training dynamics in many small firms? (Storey and Westhead, 1995; Banfield *et al*, 1996; Sadler-Smith *et al*, 1999; Jameson, 2000)

Issues of training in SMEs will be explored further in the next chapter.

BOX 6

A checklist of areas to consider for knowledge management training

- What constitutes a knowledge management culture?

- How can an organisational environment scan be undertaken?

- What helps or hinders 'knowledge mining'?

- How can information flows be mapped in order to identify the what, where and when of knowledge delivery and sharing in different contexts?

- How can points of high knowledge leverage in the informal 'shadows' of the organisation be gauged?

- How can organisational knowledge be created and identified?

- How can a culture of support for the gathering, creating and use of knowledge be created in order to keep pace with the profound changes that will affect market position?

- How can processes for defining action be identified/created?

- How can awareness be generated of how knowledge is created and used to support organisational goals?

- What tools (such as dialogic exercises and knowledge time lining) can be identified and used for determining how appropriate knowledge can be shared and disseminated?

- What should be the role of IT and information systems specialists – to provide 'information gluts', or to make it easier to gather and share, or even create, knowledge systems?

- How does valuable tacit knowledge reside in the informal networks of relationships?

- How can storytelling reach beyond the collection of easily codified information to provide a powerful way of representing different aspects of complex, multi-dimensional knowledge management activities?

- How is new knowledge created and what are the enablers and constraints of this process?

- How can customer knowledge be harnessed in order to develop customer service levels to make an organisation the provider of choice, by providing customer service training courses to respond to these?

- How can people be brought together to engage in social learning processes in decision-making forums?

- In what ways might futurist activities be harnessed (eg scenario-planning and future perfect thinking to produce knowledge that will aid in developing plans to address potential future changes in the business environment)?

- What frameworks can be used to translate knowledge into action to close the knowing–doing gap and encourage a 'felt responsibility' for specific goal-oriented steps to improve the knowledge management process?

- How can individual knowledge workers be enabled to define what they need to do back at the workplace, not only to add more value to their organisation, but also to enhance their future employability?

6 | A way forward for employers and government

◪ **Organisations will need to adopt strategies that support learning and reinforce its importance.**

◪ **Two key tasks for employers will be to motivate employees to learn, and to communicate to line managers that supporting learning and development is an essential part of their job.**

◪ **The context of small and medium-sized enterprises (SMEs) demands particular and tailored solutions to their situation in the knowledge economy.**

◪ **Skills polarisation and the demand for skills creates the need for new policies from national and supra-national bodies that support social learning and open learning markets.**

◪ **Emphasis within national VET and organisational policies needs to shift from human capital theory to the application of the concept of social capital.**

◪ **Employers will need to support informal learning, address barriers to learning and support social learning to maximise their competitive advantage.**

Employing organisations

The role of employers in relation to skills polarisation is highlighted by Rainbird (2000). Her analysis points in particular to the unequal distribution of training resources across occupational groups, with proportionately more being invested in managerial and professional groups. The CIPD training and development survey (CIPD, 2001) also clearly shows that manual workers are less likely to receive training than managerial and other professional employees. It is arguable that this arises in part from training investment being viewed as part of the managerial reward system rather than as an investment essential to organisational success. As Rainbird (2000) points out, there needs to be a closing of the gap between the rhetoric of 'people are our most important asset' and the reality of actual organisational practice.

The concept of social capital will also have value in organisations. The current interest in the application of new theories of learning as a social process has direct relevance here. These new theories – for example, that associated with the notion of 'communities of practice' – highlight the role and significance of informal and workplace learning. These learning processes seem to us to be critical in building the value of social capital in work organisations, and to be essential in knowledge creation and knowledge sharing. This is especially the case in relation to tacit knowledge and the 'knowledge spiral' suggested by Nonaka and Takeuchi (1995). Application of these new ways of understanding the relationships between

> '**Employers need to take care with decisions in relation to investment in e-learning and need to understand the use of blended learning solutions.**'

learning, knowledge and economic success will have implications for the design of work processes internal to the organisation, and for the conduct of interactions with external actors. Workplace learning also raises similar questions concerning the evaluation of training to those that apply to national policies.

A major issue for employers is the application and use of new technologies in training. As we have seen, learners do not necessarily prefer or respond positively to the use of ICT, especially when it is imposed. Use of distance learning generally requires significant investment, and this is particularly the case in relation to the use of ICT (one estimate suggests one hour of Internet-based learning requires an average of 300 hours' development at an average cost of £100 per hour). Employers need to take care with decisions in relation to investment in e-learning and need to understand the use of blended learning solutions. The use of ICT is a major factor in the emergence and operation of the knowledge economy. It does not necessarily follow that the same will be true of the training of employees.

Variability in learners' responses to ICT is only one issue that employers will need to address in relation to employee motivation. Given the changing roles and responsibilities for training and development identified in this report, it is clear that employees are expected to be more active in managing their own learning and development. However, motivation to do so cannot be taken for granted. The research evidence reviewed here suggests that motivation to manage learning is low among employees across Europe, including in the UK. Employing organisations have a major challenge here if they are to benefit from the potential offered by the knowledge economy.

A final point of significance for work organisations is addressing the training needs of employees that arise because of the knowledge economy. Our work is too limited to offer precise prescriptions. It does, however, show that roles, jobs and tasks are changing and are becoming less rather than more distinct. In addition, the role of emotion – and emotional labour in particular – will become more significant. We also report work done in retailing on future skills needs and suggest those results will have wide application. The findings of that work will therefore provide a useful starting point. Employing organisations will, however, need to pay serious attention to identifying their own specific needs.

Training in the SME environment

Small businesses make an important contribution to the development of the socio-economic and political infrastructure of industrially advanced nations (Matlay, 2000). Hill and Stewart (2000) provide an example of how SMEs can be defined, using number of employees as a variable (see Table 2).

Table 2 | European Commission's definition of SMEs from the Commission of the European Communities recommendation of 3 April 1996

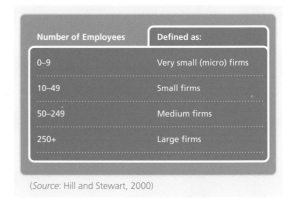

Number of Employees	Defined as:
0–9	Very small (micro) firms
10–49	Small firms
50–249	Medium firms
250+	Large firms

(*Source*: Hill and Stewart, 2000)

It has been found that the number of employees in a small business is directly correlated with the market position of the business and prevailing economic conditions (Donovan, 2000). Medium-sized companies are using new technology to improve their business, while smaller enterprises and the self-employed are falling behind in the technological revolution. A survey by Travelselect.com, a business-travel firm, found that 80 per cent of workers in medium-sized enterprises used technology 'a lot', compared with just 22 per cent of self-employed workers. Some 45 per cent of workers from the medium-sized enterprises considered that technology gave them 'a great competitive advantage'. Yet 40 per cent of self-employed workers were not using any technology at all. Around 25 per cent of those surveyed, and more than 30 per cent of those who were self-employed, said that technology would not help them succeed. Vimal Khosla, chief executive officer of Travelselect.com, argues that 'it is apparent that a significant sector of the small-business population hasn't yet woken up to the cost and labour efficiencies that technology and online purchasing can provide. Implementing change to improve one's business can be tough and is perceived as expensive but the long-term rewards of capitalising on technology can be immense. Small businesses need to realise this and act fast if they are to keep ahead' (Donovan, 2000).

It has been suggested that there is a wrong assumption about small and medium-sized enterprises (SMEs): that the training solutions benefiting larger organisations can be equally successful in smaller ones (Matlay, 1999). Training in small firms is more likely to be related to the availability, relevance and cost of training provided. It is often provided internally as a means of transferring information work skills (and the view

that absence from work could have a marked effect on productivity) rather than, like the larger firm, relying mostly upon external provision (Storey and Westhead, 1995). So different issues can be said to exist in the environment of the small and medium-sized enterprise, partly because of the size of the organisation and the tendency for on-the-job training to predominate. This reliance on informal training in SMEs, often viewed as an exclusion of staff development in a more general sense, can lead to a reduced likelihood of developing an internal labour market and increase the use of the external labour market, which enforces the vicious circle of high levels of recruitment and low levels of training (Jameson, 2000).

There are a number of skills development barriers for SMEs. First, the influence of the prevalent SME culture can be significant (if the SME is a family business, for example). Other barriers include lack of awareness of the importance of staff training and development, lack of finances, poor access to and provision of training and other skills development opportunities. Government strategies play an important part in these areas. A study on the applicability of competence-based management training and development (MTD) by Loan-Clarke *et al* (2000) revealed that the take-up of management standards in the SME sector may be failing owing to lack of awareness, and there is a major role for government-funded organisations in the promotion of standards-based training (Loan-Clarke *et al*, 2000).

However, in investigating the attitude of Scottish SMEs towards learning and skills, Lange *et al* (2000) concluded by arguing that the continuous creation of new skills strategies, new initiatives, and new (and at times misleading) names and labels in recent years has added to an apparent

> '...distance learning is more likely to have a subsidiary role in providing supporting knowledge and understanding rather than being the major force for small-business training...'

state of confusion about training and development initiatives among SME companies and their employees. Furthermore, whilst training can contribute to the relationship between organisational and managerial development (Banfield *et al*, 1996) in SMEs, strategy-making in this area is limited (Hendry *et al*, 1995), usually being done for operational, not strategic, reasons (Sadler-Smith *et al*, 1999). Therefore, whilst it has been found that the attitude of managers in SMEs towards training is generally positive, this does not translate into real provision (Matlay, 1998).

Loan-Clarke *et al* (2000) found that the topic of management training and development (MTD) in small businesses is relatively under-researched, and suggest that an increased understanding of the factors influencing the purchase of MTD by small businesses is needed. They surveyed 551 small businesses in the Midlands region of the UK in an attempt to identify influences on MTD investment and preferred MTD activities, and to establish whether small businesses perceive a link between investment in MTD and business success. Interviews were also conducted with 12 organisations. Results show that the characteristics of ownership, size, number of managers and family management have a significant influence on MTD investment. Of the sample, 85 per cent considered investment in MTD to be linked to business success, and 80 per cent of companies engaged in some form of MTD. However, promoters of MTD to small businesses need to understand that companies in this sector are not homogeneous and desire on-the-job training (Loan-Clarke *et al*, 1999). The use of e-learning and knowledge management, however, was not discussed here or in many other papers focusing on the UK to any great degree. With regard to e-learning in SMEs in the rest of the world, a study of Australian small businesses found that owners

were predominantly using the Internet as a communications medium and, to a lesser extent, as a document transfer and advertising channel (Poon and Swatman, 1997) rather than as a learning medium.

Whilst e-learning research in SMEs is in its early stages, distance learning has, however, been discussed, being suggested as one possible solution to the problem of releasing staff from the small-business site and thus ameliorating many of the logistical and operational difficulties associated with conventional training. However, it is argued that in order to be effective, small-business training must be client focused. Distance learning may be either bespoke and hence client focused or generic and arguably market focused. For SMEs, bespoke materials are too costly to develop, while generic materials may be too general to be of use in satisfying specific training needs. This limitation further supports the view that distance learning is more likely to have a subsidiary role in providing supporting knowledge and understanding rather than being the major force for small-business training that some have predicted or would like to see. For SMEs the answer to producing a viable training experience appears to be a consideration of 'blended solutions' – the carefully combined use of face-to-face and e-learning provision of training and associated materials, relevant to the business (Sadler-Smith *et al*, 1999).

One important issue raised by Sadler-Smith *et al* (1999) in their research study is that because (in their phrase) 'at-job learning' is considered to be the most desirable method of learning by SMEs, then this desire needs to be fully incorporated into any plans for providing e-learning. They also argue that greater consideration should be made of the need to give the same level of attention and development to the pedagogical as well as the technological methods of training provision in SMEs. They plea for a coherent and integrated theory of at-job learning which builds upon the action learning, management development and systemic thinking models presented by Revans (1971; 1980; 1982), Mumford (1993; 1997) and Senge (1990).

Action learning is based on Revans' 'equation' model of learning (L) = programmed knowledge (P) + the ability to ask insightful questions (Q). Action learning assists individuals who are working with others to solve 'real' work problems as a group and consciously learn from the experience. Kolb's experiential learning cycle (Kolb, 1984) also provides a framework for reflection, abstraction and action planning. The critical incident review approach is another mechanism by which significant events can form an input to the reflective process in an individual or group learning context. The challenge is to integrate and further develop existing techniques, such as action learning and critical incident review, into a coherent 'pedagogy and method' of client-focused at-job learning. Distance learning, along with other methods, may have an important role as supporting media (Sadler-Smith *et al*, 2000).

National policy-makers
Skills-development policy implications

The emergence and growth of the knowledge economy has led to the design of a number of skills-development policies by national governments and supra-national agencies. Green (2000) identifies two broad approaches. The first is termed the wide skills distribution model; Germany and Japan are cited as examples of where this approach has been adopted. The model promotes small scientific and engineering élites with a wide distribution of intermediate skills. In contrast, the USA and the UK are said to have adopted an alternative model, which Green terms the 'high skills élite model'. Here, intermediate skills are not promoted and the skills base is 'polarised' between the élite and those with low or no skills.

A central issue in every industrialised country is therefore the manner in which the education and training systems can be improved and skills developed. According to this convention, once you have more and better skills, prosperity will follow. But Ashton and Green (1996) suggest that the high-skills route is not possible for all countries. They argue that a period of relatively successful economic growth and development lasting at least a decade based on the predominant use of high-level skills in high-value-added production technologies is necessary for successful pursuit of the high-skills route. In addition, not all countries are converging towards a common modern technology in which ever-increasing and broader skills are needed, and there are differences in the skills demanded and supplied. Furthermore, education and training systems are relatively autonomous and there is international variation in the quality of education. The authors therefore warn that simplistic borrowing from the policies of relatively successful countries is unlikely to result in success.

Each of these models is related to the competition strategies adopted and promoted by the respective governments, and so, in the UK, for example, the model follows a mixed strategy of supporting high-technology/high-skill sectors with strategies focusing on low cost/flexible labour in other sectors. An example of the former is the UK government's initiative in relation to e-commerce (see www.dti.gov.uk). In the latter case, we also see changes in the employment contract and management practices, but perhaps not of the nature suggested by Bentley (1998).

> **'If knowledge and its creation are at the centre of the economy, then economic actors need to be engaged in continuous learning.'**

In spite of these apparent developments, however, it is debatable whether they have been appropriate or sufficient. Field (2000) calls for new institutional structures, perhaps echoing the WER's (2001) conclusions that 'the values, agreements and institutions of an earlier industrial era are often no longer suited to current trends in working conditions' (p12).

The knowledge economy and the learning society

Green (2000) argues that globalisation creates increased demands for learning to generate the skills necessary for economic success and the competences required to promote social cohesion. The WER (2001) lends further support to this by suggesting that education is the key to ensuring economic and social benefits from the knowledge economy. In support of both these views, Richardson and Unwin (2000) suggest that there is a clear connection between the notion of a 'learning society' and a knowledge economy.

These arguments require a brief examination of the term 'learning society' (LS) and its close relative, 'lifelong learning' (LLL). The notion of an LS is simply one where adult citizens continue to engage in learning. The connection with LLL is therefore clear. An LS is populated by lifelong learners. This is perhaps a crude caricature, for as Field (2000) points out, both concepts are subject to varying interpretations. However, the description does convey the essence of the concepts.

Both the European Union (EU) and the UK government have applied these concepts as part of their competition policies (Field, 2000). From a policy perspective, both the attraction and the purpose of the concepts have been in relation to competitive advantage and economic success. This emphasis has been criticised by a number of academics and commentators (see Field, 2000). Whatever the merits of those critiques, LLL has recently been confirmed as part of EU policy (EU, 2001).

The connection with the knowledge economy is also fairly obvious. If knowledge and its creation are at the centre of the economy, then economic actors need to be engaged in continuous learning. At the organisational level, this requires applying ideas such as those developed by Dixon (1998). There are, though, two problems. The policies pursued under the banner of LLL have placed the individual in the centre as a learner. As Dixon (1998) argues in her work on organisational learning, this misses the collective and social character of learning. It has also had the effect of commodifying learning, with the result that the individual is treated as a consumer (see Green, 2000). But, as both Green (2001) and the WER (2001) point out, the learning market is not inclusive.

One of the key tasks the government's Learning and Skills Council has set for itself is to increase demand for learning by adults and equalise opportunities through better access to learning (Learning and Skills Council, 2001). But there are problems with the current approach. First, initiatives focus on the individual, when evidence suggests the need for more support of collaborative learning. Part of the explanation for policy initiatives focusing on the individual is the dominant influence of human capital theory (see Rees, 2000).

This is linked to the second problem. If knowledge creation depends on collaborative networks, then investment in (individual) human capital will not promote the very factor of production and basis of competitive advantage necessary for competitive success. Recent initiatives such as learndirect have harnessed the power of technology to deliver learning to those who would otherwise not have access, but they tend to focus on helping people use e-learning to train themselves, rather than support the development of social learning networks.

Third, the problem of the closed learning market persists. Government-sponsored initiatives tend to focus on basic skills, but there are fewer opportunities for those requiring training in intermediate skills. Employers are dedicating most of their training spend to knowledge workers and management, leaving a gap between where government-sponsored training begins, employer-sponsored training trails off, and where individuals trying to build up intermediate skills can afford to purchase training for themselves. Individual Learning Accounts were perhaps a partial attempt to help bridge this gap but, as their failure demonstrates, finding solutions to this problem will not be easy.

It is these arguments on the nature of the learning market that lead Green (2000), among others, to argue for different forms of state intervention, and those on the nature of the knowledge economy that led Field (2000), among others, to call for the application of the notion of social capital in those interventions.

7 | Summary and future research

◩ **Government, employers and the training profession need to work separately and together to encourage positive attitudes towards learning.**

◩ **The role of the line manager is of major importance in supporting learning. Helping managers to understand this responsibility and to support learners is a key task of the training profession in the knowledge economy.**

◩ **Collaborative learning through internal and external networks and communities of interest are a key feature of learning in the knowledge economy.**

◩ **Managing learning for knowledge workers requires flexible approaches – training professionals can help to motivate learners by helping to align corporate and individual learning goals, and by providing flexible learning delivery and design to meet individual needs.**

◩ **New approaches to learning signal a shift away from instruction towards facilitation.**

◩ **E-learning is unlikely to provide a single or universal solution to meeting learning needs.**

The challenges of learning and training in the knowledge economy cannot be met by training professionals alone. Government, employers and the training profession will need to work together to encourage positive attitudes towards learning, to increase motivation, and to develop flexible new approaches to learning, particularly through the development of networks of collaboration that take into account the importance of social capital. New approaches to learning that build on this collaborative approach will mean a shift away from a focus on instruction to one of facilitation in both organisational and national policies. It will also require greater awareness of cross-cultural issues and individual learning preferences.

Training specialists are facing many challenges in the knowledge economy, which also presents new and valuable opportunities. The importance of knowledge and learning in economic success should put training and the work of training specialists centre stage. This will happen, though, only if the opportunities presented by the focus on knowledge and learning are taken. In light of this, training specialists need to pay attention to playing their role in identifying the needs just mentioned. They also need to ensure that they meet their own needs for professional development. Those suggested previously in this report will be a useful starting point for the diagnosis of personal and individual needs.

> **'A major challenge for training specialists lies in overcoming negative attitudes towards learning.'**

The role of training specialists is changing. They will be expected to be a source of expertise and advice in, for example, the use of ICT in training and the design of blended learning in particular. Given the strategic importance of knowledge and learning, especially in relation to intellectual and emotional labour rather than physical labour, training specialists can expect to provide a more strategic contribution in the future (see also Tjepkema et al, 2002).

A major challenge for training specialists lies in overcoming negative attitudes towards learning. Another challenge will be how to promote and encourage informal learning within the workplace on the part of line and operational managers. A third challenge will lie in demonstrating to senior management the absolute necessity for them to take responsibility for and encourage learning in both formal and informal aspects.

In all cases, the application of new methods and techniques that reflect theories of learning as a social process, and that promote the development of social capital, may be resisted. This is because such methods and techniques will require much more active involvement from non-managerial employees and managers alike. Training specialists will need to be prepared to meet this challenge. To do this, training professionals will need to give learners more choice in learning approaches and modes of delivery (traditional, experiential, e-learning and a mix of instruction-based, cognitive and social learning models), maintain an awareness of changing employment structures for themselves and their clients, encourage win–win learning partnerships (between a company and university for example), work towards aligning company objectives with the learning goals of employees, and encourage the development of management competencies for supporting learning and development.

A knowledge economy must invest in people and their training and education. The purpose, focus and nature of those investments are both difficult and contentious questions. Our review suggests some possible answers. One overarching point is that many of the studies included in our review share a view that institutional change is required, and that this must encompass institutions involved in vocational education and training (see Bjornavold, 2000; Field, 2000; and WER, 2001). Such changes should reflect the network dynamic of the knowledge economy itself, and therefore cross-sector collaboration needs to be encouraged. Given the importance of the SME sector to the national economy, training needs must be identified and supported via government initiatives.

Skills polarisation seems to be of increasing concern in the EU and the UK (IPTS, 2000; WER, 2001; Field, 2000). This is in part an outcome of an overemphasis on the supply side of the labour market in national policies (Field, 2000; Rainbird, 2000) which, in turn, can be associated with competition policies (Green, 2000). It is also associated with the influence of human capital theory in national policies (Rees, 2000). A significant outcome of skills polarisation causing concern is the effect on social cohesion. It seems from our analysis that the application of social capital theory in national policies in relation to vocational education and training would promise some success in overcoming both skills polarisation and its effects on social cohesion.

A related point is an overemphasis on the economic and measurable effects of policy interventions, especially in their evaluation. As Grubb and Ryan (2000) argue in their analysis, evaluation techniques such as cost/benefit analysis fail to take account of, or value, the social benefits of policy interventions related to training. Application of social capital theory would provide an impetus to the development and application of more relevant techniques which both recognise and value social and cultural as well as strictly economic outcomes.

All of these points are in part reflective of an emphasis on the individual as the focus of policy. We have seen, though, that individuals can and do display low levels of motivation to accept responsibility for learning (Rainbird, 2000; Sambrook, 2001; Tjepkema et al, 2002).

Policy-makers in government and employing organisations will need to address these and other pressing issues. Perhaps most urgent is the problem of a potential gap between an expectation of individual responsibility for learning and low levels of employee motivation to manage their own continuous learning in and through work.

Future research

In closing their edited collection of current research in HRD, McGoldrick et al (2002) identify a number of issues that they argue will constitute the future research agenda. These include the following:

◻ *Learning processes* – There is a need for more research into how learning occurs and how it can be facilitated. This applies to group or team and organisational levels as well as to individual processes.

◻ *Purpose and accountability of HRD* – The traditional focus of performance, of both individual jobholders and organisations, no longer fully explains or justifies investment in HRD. Related to this, HRD practice seems to be accountable to a wider constituency than just organisational decision-makers. Research is needed on the extent and implications of these developments.

◻ *HRD in the business environment* – Changes in the business environment – globalisation for example – will have implications for HRD practice. More needs to be known and understood about these implications.

◻ *Work organisation and design* – The nature of work and its design is clearly changing. The rise of what is termed 'emotional labour' to replace the physical labour of the 'old' economy is one example. Research is needed to better understand these changes and how HRD practice is responding now and needs to respond in the future.

◻ *Individual identity* – Careers, jobs and professions have long been recognised as being central to the construction of individual identity. However, all of these are changing and, therefore, so too is their role in individual identities. HRD plays a central and critical role in career and professional as well as personal development, but the connections between that role and the construction of identity are not well understood. Research is needed, therefore, on the role of HRD in the context of more unstable and fluid careers and professions.

All of these issues for future research are reinforced by the analysis in this report. Research into learning processes, accountabilities of training, the connections between global change and training practice, the organisation and design of work and the role of training in the construction of individual identity will inform and increase understanding of the implications of the knowledge economy for training practice. The agenda set out above is therefore relevant and appropriate to the findings of this report.

Much work is being done, for example the research into learning processes recently published by the CIPD (Caley *et al*, 2002). The CIPD annual *Training Survey* also includes questions of relevance to training in the knowledge economy. The authors cited in the text and those listed in the References here (pp55–9) are also currently engaged in relevant research that addresses some of the issues detailed above. However, two issues remain largely unaddressed. The first is that much, or even most, of the current research adopts a labour market perspective. This in turn has two consequences. First, a focus on national policy interventions rather than on one that examines the detail of organisational and professional practice. Second, an overemphasis on quantitative methodologies. We agree with McGoldrick *et al* (2001) in their call for more interpretative studies.

The second issue is that of the voice of training specialists. Much research focuses on the views of policy makers at national and organisational levels. In some cases, the focus is on the user or client of training interventions, ie 'the learner'. This situation misses the experience and knowledge of training specialists themselves. There are of course exceptions to this assertion – the ETV and CIPD surveys, for example. There remains, though, a need for research that focuses on and engages the experience of training specialists. Of particular importance is using such research to fill the major gap in knowledge on the development needs associated with the knowledge-based economy of training specialists themselves. Research projects that adopt interpretative methodologies and that engage with the experience of practitioners will

help us to better understand the impact and implications of the knowledge economy on and for training practice.

Appendix 1

Methodology

In addressing the aims of the research, this report relied on the following four-part framework to focus on the main issues:

- changes in the business environment, the organisation of work and individual and organisational learning

- the impact of these changes on learner behaviour, the management of learning, the training professions' customer base and the role of training professionals

- lessons for the future of training and development

- issues and implications arising from the report.

Desk-based methods were adopted, so there was a reliance on an analysis of existing literature. Readers can therefore gain a reasonable knowledge of the availability of recent and current research. However, the timescales allocated to the project did not allow for a review of all of the available literature. Instead, the method used was to select sources judged to be most helpful and representative. The report most relies on these sources in the text.

Appendix 2

Glossary of terms

Communities of practice – consist of networks of people who work together in an organisation and who regularly share information and knowledge. Such people may be, but are not necessarily, part of formal teams or units. They often collaborate on particular projects or products, or they hold the same or similar jobs. They have been described as 'peers in the execution of real work'. Communities of practice are held together by shared goals and a need to learn from each other (Seely Brown and Solomon Gray, 1997).

E-learning – 'learning that is delivered, enabled or mediated by electronic technology for the explicit purpose of training in organisations. It does not include stand-alone technology-based training such as the use of CD-ROMs in isolation' (www.cipd.co.uk).

Enterprise resource planning (ERP) systems – based on developing a common IT infrastructure and common business processes, these provide a means of integrating the core corporate activities of an enterprise, such as finance, logistics and human resources. They provide for the identification of the organisation's resources and the application of them in the most effective manner to fulfil the business objectives. Developed in response to the need to manage across global businesses (which is difficult when each business is using different systems and technologies), ERP is therefore claimed to be a business solution implemented to support the integration of business activity (Newell *et al*, 2001).

Globalisation – denotes a growing interdependence of world society (Giddens, 1989).

Informal learning – learning that occurs outside planned and explicit learning interventions.

Innovation – Van de Ven (in Cooper and Argyris, 1998) defines an innovation as the creation and implementation of a new idea that may be technological (new technical artefacts, devices or products), a process (new services, programs or production procedures) or administrative (new institutional policies, structures or systems). He suggests that the idea may be a novel recombination of old ideas, a scheme that challenges the present order, or an unprecedented formula or approach, but as long as the idea is perceived as new and entails a novel change for those involved, it is an innovation.

Knowledge – Nonaka *et al* adopt what they describe as the traditional definition of knowledge as 'justified true belief' (2002, p42). They elaborate the definition by emphasising the dynamic, contextual and social nature of knowledge and its creation. They also usefully distinguish between two types of knowledge: explicit and tacit. Explicit knowledge can be directly expressed and communicated in the form of data, specifications and manuals, whereas tacit knowledge is personal and difficult to articulate. Nonaka and his colleagues suggest insights, intuitions and hunches as examples of tacit knowledge.

Knowledge economy – is different from the new economy in a number of ways, not least the recognition of the importance of know-how, innovation, design and branding to the generation of a firm's competitive advantage and the social processes that create these.

Knowledge-intensive firm – where work is said to be of an intellectual nature and where well-educated, highly qualified employees form the major part of the workforce.

Knowledge management (KM) – Swan and Newell (1994) suggest that KM relates to any process or practice that involves acquiring and using knowledge to enhance organisational performance. Moreover, KM processes are concerned with ensuring that once knowledge is acquired and used at one place and one time to solve a particular problem, this should be captured and shared so that the knowledge embedded in the solution can be reused at other places and times. KM is therefore obviously intimately related to issues of organisational learning (or the learning organisation), which is also about ensuring learning accumulates over time within an organisation. The focus of KM is therefore to better leverage the intellectual capital that resides within organisational innovation processes.

New economy – describes the transformation of economic activities that is taking place as digital technologies make the accessing, processing and storage of information increasingly cheaper and easier. (Commission for European Communities, 2000)

Social capital – 'the sum of actual and potential resources within, available through, and derived from the network of relationships possessed by an individual or social unit. Social capital thus comprises both the network and the assets that may be mobilized through the network' (Nahapiet and Ghoshal, 1998, p243).

Training – has traditionally been defined as consisting of formal or informal group or individual learning experiences designed to impart or improve employees' skills, competency, knowledge and/or job performance (Stewart, 1996).

Training and development function – has been described as having 'the aim of ensuring that the contribution of individuals and groups to the agreement and achievement of organisation objectives is maximized through the development of appropriate knowledge, skills and attitudes. Its contribution to organisational performance and effectiveness is primarily through the development of people as individuals, as work groups and as members of the wider organization' (Stewart, 1996).

Workplace learning – the CIPD (2000, p2) defines workplace learning as those 'activities [that] include all the formal and non-formal training, instruction and coaching activities that go on, partly or wholly, in the workplace'.

References

ADAMS E. C. and FREEMAN C. (2000)

'Communities of practice: bridging technology and knowledge assessment'. *Journal of Knowledge Management*. Vol. 4, No. 1. pp38–44.

ALVESSON M. (1993)

'Organisations as rhetoric: knowledge-intensive firms and the struggle with ambiguity'. *Journal of Management Studies*. Vol. 30, No. 6.

ALVESSON M. (1995)

Management of Knowledge-Intensive Companies. Berlin, de Gruyter.

ANTONACOPOULOU E. and GABRIEL Y. (2001)

'Emotion, learning and organisational change: towards an integration of psychoanalytic and other perspectives'. *Journal of Organizational Change Management*. Vol. 14, No. 5.

ARGYRIS C. and SCHON D. (1978)

Organisational Learning. Reading, Mass., Addison Wesley.

ASHTON D. and GREEN F. (1996)

Education, Training and the Global Economy. London, Edward Elgar.

BANFIELD P., JENNINGS P. L. and BEAVER G. (1996)

'Competence-based training for small firms – an expensive failure?' *Long Range Planning*. Vol. 29, No. 1. pp94–102.

BARNETT R. (2000)

Working Knowledge: Research and knowledge at work. London, Routledge.

BARRIE J. and PACE R. W. (1997)

'Competence, efficiency and organizational learning'. *Human Resource Development Quarterly*. Vol. 8, No. 4. pp335–42.

BASSI L. J. (1997)

'Harnessing the power of intellectual capital'. *Training and Development*. December.

BEAUJOLIN F. (1997)

Technological and Economic Issues Related to the Future of Work. Study for the European Commission.

BENTLEY T. (1998)

Learning beyond the Classroom: Education for a changing world. London, Routledge.

BJORNAVOLD J. (2000)

Making Learning Visible: Identification, assessment and recognition of non-formal learning in Europe. Thessaloniki, CEDEFOP.

BOLLINGER A. S. and SMITH R. D. (2001)

'Managing organizational knowledge as a strategic asset'. *Journal of Knowledge Management*. Vol. 5, No. 1. pp8–18.

BOUCHER P. (2001)

'BA gains e-HR project feedback via Net game'. *Personnel Today*. www.personneltoday.com/pt_news/ news_daily_det.asp?liArticleID=7984

BROWNING J. and REISS S. (2001)

'Encyclopedia of the new economy'. hotwired.lycos.com/special/ene/. 10 August.

CALEY L., MASON R. and REYNOLDS J. (2002)

How Do People Learn? London, CIPD.

CASTELLS M. (1996)

The Rise of the Network Society. Oxford, Blackwell.

CIPD (1999)

Organisational Development – Whose responsibility? London, CIPD.

CIPD (2000)

Success through Learning: The argument for strengthening workplace learning. London, CIPD.

CIPD (2001)

Training and Development 2001. Survey Report. London, CIPD.

CIPD (2002)

Who Learns at Work? Survey Report. London, CIPD.

COLEMAN J. S. (1998)

'Social capital in the creation of human capital'. *American Journal of Sociology*. Vol. 94. pp s95–s120.

COMMISSION OF THE EUROPEAN COMMUNITIES (2000)

eEurope: An information society for all. Progress Report for the Special European Council on Employment, Economic Reforms and Social Cohesion – Towards a Europe Based on Innovation and Knowledge. Lisbon, 23 and 24 March, Brussels, COM (2000) 130 final.

COOPER C. and ARGYRIS C. (1998)

The Concise Blackwell Encyclopedia of Management. Oxford, Blackwell.

COPE N. (2001)

'Whatever happened to one-time Internet darling Freeserve?' *The Independent*. 16 November.

COULSON-THOMAS C. (1999)

'Individuals and enterprise: developing intrapreneurs for the new millennium'. *Industrial and Commercial Training*. Vol. 31, No. 7. pp258–61.

CRICK B. (2000)

Learning: Right or responsibility? The learning society and the knowledge economy. Coventry, National Advisory Council for Education and Training Targets lecture series.

DANIEL J. (1999)

Mega-Universities and Knowledge Media: Technology strategies for higher education. London, Kogan Page.

DAUM J. (2001)

'New new economy management best practice – the competence center for intangible assets-based management techniques and systems'. www.juergendaum.com/. 16 July.

DIXON N. (1998)

The Organisational Learning Cycle: How we can learn collectively. Aldershot, Gower.

DIXON N. (2000)

Common Knowledge. Boston, Harvard Business School Press.

DONOVAN P. (2000)

'Small and imperfectly informed: small businesses and self-employed workers are failing to reap the benefits of the technological revolution'. www.peoplemanagement.co.uk/archive/2000/16_Oct/special/it2.asp.

DRUCKER P. (1993)

Post-Capitalist Society. Oxford, Butterworth-Heinemann.

ECCLESTONE K. and FIELD J. (2001)

Promoting Social Capital in a Risk Society. EERA European Conference on Educational Research, Charles de Gaulle University, Lille, France.

EUROPEAN COMMISSION (2000)

eEurope: An information society for all. Progress Report for the Special European Council on Employment, Economic Reforms and Social Cohesion – Towards a Europe Based on Innovation and Knowledge. Lisbon, 23 and 24 March 2000. Brussels. COM (2000) 130 final. 2000.

EUROPEAN COMMISSION (2001)

Employment in Europe 2001: Recent trends and prospects. Luxembourg, EC.

FIELD J. (2000)

Lifelong Learning and the New Educational Order. Stoke-on-Trent, Trentham Books.

FINEMAN S. (ED.) (1993)

Emotion in Organisation. London, Sage.

GIDDENS A. (1989)

Sociology. Cambridge, Polity Press.

GRANDORI A. and SODA G. (1995)

'Interfirm networks: antecedents, mechanisms and forms'. *Organization Studies*. Vol. 16. pp183–214.

GREEN A. (2000)

Education, Globalisation and the Nation State: The learning society and the knowledge economy. Coventry, National Advisory Council for Education and Training Targets lecture series.

GRUBB W. N. and RYAN R. (2000)

The Roles of Evaluation for VET: Plain talk on the field of dreams. Geneva, International Labour Organisation.

HARRISON R. (2000)

Employee Development. London, CIPD.

HENDRY C., ARTHUR M. B. and JONES A. (1995)

Strategy through People: Adaptation and learning in the small–medium enterprise. London, Routledge.

HILL R. and STEWART J. (2000)

'Human resource development in small organizations'. *Journal of European Industrial Training*. Vol. 24, No. 2. pp105–17.

HISLOP D., NEWELL S., SWAN J. and SCARBROUGH H. (1997)

'Innovation and networks: linking diffusion and implemenation'. *International Journal of Innovation Management*. Vol. 4, No. 1. pp427–48.

HOCHSCHILD A. R. (1983)

The Managed Heart: Commercialisation of human feeling. Berkeley, University of California Press.

INSTITUTE FOR PROSPECTIVE TECHNOLOGICAL STUDIES (2000)

The IPTS Futures Project Conference Proceedings. Brussels.

INTERNATIONAL LABOUR OFFICE (2001)

World Employment Report 2001 – Life at work in the information economy. Geneva, ILO.

JAMESON S. M. (2000)

'Recruitment and training in small firms'. *Journal of European Industrial Training.* Vol. 24, No. 1. pp43–9.

KAPLAN R. S. and NORTON D. P. (1996)

The Balanced Scorecard. Boston, Harvard Business School Press.

KLEIN N. (2000)

No Logo, No Space, No Choice, No Jobs: Taking an aim at the bullies' brands. London, Flamingo.

KNOWLES V. and STEWART J. (2001)

'Graduate recruitment: implications for business and management courses in HE'. *Journal of European Industrial Training.* Vol. 25, No. 2.

KOLB D. (1984)

Experiential Learning. Englewood Cliffs, N.J., Prentice Hall.

KOTOROV R. and HSU E. (2001)

'A model for enterprise portal management'. *Journal of Knowledge Management.* Vol. 5, No. 1. pp86–93.

LANGE T., OTTENS M. and TAYLOR A. (2000)

'SMEs and barriers to skills development: a Scottish perspective'. *Journal of European Industrial Training.* Vol. 24, No. 1. pp5–11.

LANK E. (1998)

'Café society'. *People Management.* Vol. 4, No. 4. pp40–43.

LEADBEATER C. (2000)

Living on Thin Air: The new economy. London, Viking.

LEANA C. R. (1999)

'Organizational social capital and employment practices'. *Academy of Management Review.* July.

LEARNING AND SKILLS COUNCIL (2001)

Strategic Framework to 2004. London, LSC.

LEGGE K. (1995)

Human Resource Management: Rhetorics and realities. London, Macmillan.

LOAN-CLARKE J., BOOCOCK G. and SMITH A. (2000)

'Competence-based management development in small and medium-sized enterprises: a multi-stakeholder analysis'. *International Journal of Training and Development.* Vol. 4, No. 3. pp176–95.

MALHOTRA Y. (2000)

'Knowledge assets in the global economy: assessment of national intellectual capital'. *Journal of Global Information Management.* Vol. 8, No. 3. July–Sept. pp5–15.

MANN S. (1997)

'Emotional labour in organizations'. *Leadership and Organizational Development Journal.* Vol. 18, No. 1. pp4–12.

MATLAY H. (1998)

'The paradox of training in the small business sector of the British economy'. *Journal of Vocational Education and Training.* Vol. 49, No. 1. pp6–13.

MATLAY H. (1999)

'Vocational education and training in Britain: a small business perspective'. *Education and Training.* Vol. 41, No. 1. pp6–13.

MATLAY H. (2000)

'Vocational education and training in small businesses: setting a research agenda for the twenty-first century'. *Education and Training.* Vol. 42, No. 4/5. pp200–1.

McGOLDRICK J., STEWART J. and WATSON S. (2002)

Understanding Human Resource Development: A research-based approach. London, Routledge.

MEISTER J. (1998)

Corporate Universities. New York, McGraw-Hill.

MILLER L., RANKIN N. and NEATHEY F. (2002)

Competency Frameworks in UK Organisations. London, Chartered Institute of Personnel and Development.

MILLER R. and STEWART J. (1999)

'Opened University: Unipart as a learning organisation'. *People Management.* Vol. 5, No. 12.

MORI (1998)

Attitudes for Learning '98. Campaign for Learning, MORI State of the Nation survey.

MUMFORD A. (1997)

Management Development: Strategies for action. London, IPD.

NAHAPIET J. and GHOSHAL S. (1998)

'Social capital, intellectual capital and the organizational advantage'. *Academy of Management Review*. Vol. 23, No. 2. pp242–66.

NEWELL S., TANSLEY C. and HUANG J. (2001)

Knowledge Creation in an ERP Project Team: The unexpected debilitating impact of social capital. Boston, Mass., Enterprise Systems Track, Americas Conference on Information Systems (AMCIS), University of Bentley.

NONAKA I. (1994)

'A dynamic theory of organisational knowledge creation'. *Organization Science*. Vol. 5, No. 1. pp14–37.

NONAKA I. and NISHIGUCHI T. (2000)

Knowledge Emergence. Oxford, Oxford University Press.

NONAKA I. and TAKEUCHI H. (1995)

The Knowledge-Creating Company. Oxford, Oxford University Press.

NONAKA I., TOYAMA R. and KONNO N. (2002)

'SECI, Ba and leadership: a unified model of dynamic knowledge creation'. In S. Little, P. Quintas and T. Ray (eds) *Managing Knowledge: An essential reader*. London, Sage. pp41–67.

PHILLIPS J. J. (1999)

HRD Trends Worldwide: Shared solutions to compete in a global economy. Houston, Tex., Gulf Publishing Company.

PILEMER F. and RACIOPPO S. (1999)

'A structure for collaboration'. *The Alliance Analyst*. December.

POON S. and SWATMAN P. M. C. (1997)

'Small business use of the Internet: findings from Australian case studies'. *International Marketing Review*. Vol. 14, No. 5. pp385–402.

PRINCE C. and STEWART J. (UNDER REVIEW).

'Corporate Universities: an analytical framework'. *Management Learning*.

PUTNAM R. (1993)

Demoracy and the Civic Community. New Jersey, Princeton University Press.

PUTNAM R. (2000)

Bowling Alone: The collapse and revival of American community. New York, Simon & Schuster.

RAFAILI A. and SUTTON R. I. (1987)

'Expression of emotion as part of the work role'. *Academy of Management Review*. Vol. 12, No. 1. pp23–37.

RAINBIRD H. (2000)

The Contribution of Workplace Learning to a Learning Society. The Learning Society and the Knowledge Economy, Coventry, National Advisory Council for Education and Training Targets lecture series.

REES G. (2000)

Can a 'Learning Society' Produce a Knowledge Economy? The Learning Society and the Knowledge Economy, Coventry, National Advisory Council for Education and Training Targets lecture series.

REVANS R. W. (1971)

Developing Effective Managers. London, Longman.

REVANS R. W. (1980)

Action Learning. London, Blond and Briggs.

REVANS R. W. (1982)

Origins and Growth of Action Learning. Bromley, Chartwell Bratt.

RICHARDSON W. and UNWIN L. (2000)

Introduction. The Learning Society and the Knowledge Economy, Coventry, National Advisory Council for Education and Training Targets lecture series.

RIFKIN J. (1995)

The End of Work. New York, GP Putnam's Sons.

RITZER G. (2000)

The McDonaldization of Society. London, Sage.

ROBERTSON R. (1992)

Globalization: Social theory and global culture. London, Sage.

RUGMAN A. (2001)

The End of Globalization. London, Random House Business Books.

SADLER-SMITH E., DOWN S. and FIELD J. (1999)

'Adding value to HRD: evaluation, Investors in People and small firm training'. *Human Resource Development International*. Vol. 2, No. 4. pp369–90.

SADLER-SMITH E., DOWN S. and LEAN J. (2000)

'"Modern" learning methods: rhetoric and reality'. *Personnel Review*. Vol. 29, No. 4. pp474–90.

SAMBROOK S. (2001)

'Developing a model of factors influencing work-related learning: findings from two research projects'. EERA European Conference on Educational Research, Charles de Gaulle University, Lille, France.

SAMBROOK S., GEERTSHUIS S. and CHESELDINE D. V. (2001)

'Developing a quality assurance system for computer-based learning materials – problems and issues'. *Assessment and Evaluation in Higher Education*. Vol. 26, No. 5.

SCARBROUGH H., SWAN J. A. and PRESTON, J. (1998)

Knowledge Management and the Learning Organisation. London, Institute of Personnel and Development.

SCHON D. A. (1987)

Educating the Reflective Practitioner. San Francisco, Jossey-Bass.

SEELY BROWN J. and SOLOMON GRAY E. (1997)

The People Are the Company, Fast Company.

SENGE P. (1990)

'The leader's new work: building learning organisations'. *Sloan Management Review*. Vol. 32. Fall. pp9–10.

SENIOR C. (2001)

'Internet-based professional development project report produced for the Interprofessional CPD Forum as part of the United Kingdom Interprofessional Group'. DfEE Workplace Learning Division.

SLOMAN M. (2001a)

The E-Learning Revolution. London, CIPD.

SLOMAN M. (2001b)

'The state of the E-nation – a UK trainer makes some observations about US e-learning'. *Training and Development*. August. Vol. 55, No. 8. pp61–2.

SMIDT L. T. (1999)

'Use of information technology in adult education'. In J. Field (ed.) *Lifelong Learning and the New Educational Order*. Stoke-on-Trent, Trentham Books.

STEWART J. (1996)

Managing Change through Training and Development. London, Kogan Page.

STOREY D. and WESTHEAD P. (1995)

'Management training in small firms: a case of market failure?' Working paper no. 29, Small and Medium Enterprises Centre, University of Warwick.

SWAN J. and NEWELL S. (1994)

'Managers' beliefs about factors affecting the adoption of technological innovation'. *Journal of Management Psychology*. Vol. 9. pp3–11.

TAYLOR S. (1998)

'Emotional labour and the new workplace'. In P. Thompson and C. Warhurst (eds) *Workplaces of the Future*. Basingstoke, Macmillan Press Ltd.

THE ECONOMIST (1999)

'A price on the priceless'. 12–18 June. p72.

THE ECONOMIST (2001).

'Lessons of a virtual timetable'. 17 February. p101.

TJEPKEMA S., STEWART J., SAMBROOK S., MULDER M., TER HORST H. and SCHEERENS J. (EDS) (2002)

HRD and Learning Organisations in Europe. HRD Research Monograph Series. London, Routledge.

VAN MAANEN J. and KUNDA G. (1989)

'Real-feelings; emotional expression and organisational culture'. In L. L. Cummings and J. Straw (eds) *Research in Organisational Behaviour*. Greenwich, Conn., JAI Press.

WATSON T. (1999)

'Human resourcing strategies: choice, chance and circumstances'. In J. Leopold, L. Harris and T. Watson (eds) *Strategic Human Resourcing: Principles, perspectives and practices in HRM*. London, FT Management.

WER (2001) – SEE INTERNATIONAL LABOUR OFFICE (2001).

WILSON D., LANK E., WESTWOOD A., KEEP E., LEADBEATER C. and SLOMAN M. (2001)

The Future of Learning for Work. London, Chartered Institute of Personnel and Development.

ZENGER J. and UEHLEIN C. (2001)

'Why blended will win'. *Training and Development*. Vol. 55, No. 8. pp54–60.